D0859526

ISLANDS AT THE EDGE

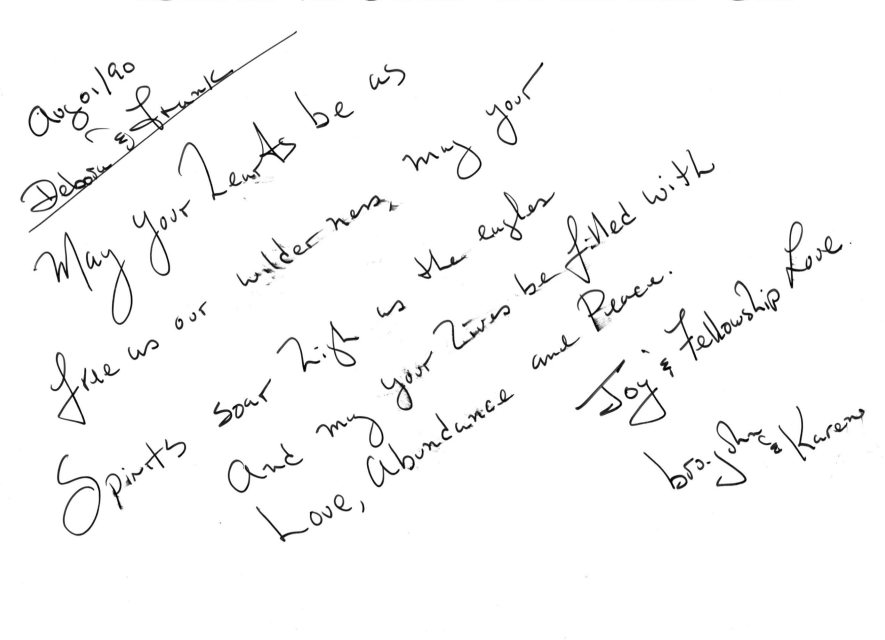

Aug 01/90
Deborah & Frank

May your hearts be as
free as our wilderness, may your
Spirits soar lift as the eagles
And may your lives be filled with
Love, Abundance and Peace.

Joy & Fellowship Love.

650-John & Karen

Queen Charlotte Summer in Skidegate Channel, 1983 — Takao Tanabe

ISLANDS AT THE EDGE

Preserving the Queen Charlotte Islands Wilderness

Islands Protection Society

Douglas & McIntyre
Vancouver/Toronto

©1984 by Islands Protection Society on behalf of the individual contributors
88   5

All rights reserved. No part of this book may be reproduced or transmitted in any form by any means without permission in writing from the publisher, except by a reviewer, who may quote brief passages in a review.

Douglas & McIntyre Ltd., 1615 Venables Street,
Vancouver, British Columbia V5L 2H1

Canadian Cataloguing in Publication Data
Main entry under title:
Islands at the edge
Bibliography: p.
ISBN 0-88894-425-X
1. Natural history – British Columbia – Queen
Charlotte Islands. 2. Queen Charlotte Islands (B.C.)
– Description and travel. 3. Nature conservation –
British Columbia – Queen Charlotte Islands.
4. Moresby Island (B.C.) I. Islands Protection
Society.
QH106.2.B8I84 1984 574.9711'31 C84-091228-5

Design by Broadhead, Henley & Associates
Maps, pages 18, 19 by John Broadhead
Logo: Bear Emerging from Cave by Bill Reid
Printed and bound in Hong Kong by Colorcraft

*This book and our efforts are
dedicated to the islands and the
earth, the little ones and the unborn.*

*Pages 6–7: view of the San Cristoval Range
looking south, the open Pacific blanketed by fog.*

CONTENTS

FOREWORD

When my friends from the Islands Protection Society asked me to write this preface, I hesitated at first for quite a long time. Never having had the opportunity to go myself to the Queen Charlotte Islands, was I entitled to write about them? All my life, I have only described spectacles I have observed myself, only made comments drawn from personal observations and only formed conclusions dictated by prolonged study of those things which I could see with my own eyes. This attitude is not dictated by a sense of my own importance but by the need I feel to see things clearly and as they are. Although the destiny of the Queen Charlotte Islands has been threatened, for over ten years now a devoted, competent and stubborn crew of scientists has been working on their behalf. This beautiful book bears witness to the labours of those scientists. Why, then, do I go today against the rule I have always followed?

It would be difficult to date exactly when I became personally aware of the fatal duality common to the islands of the world. All are at the same time extremely fragile and extremely precious. This dual characteristic unites them as surely as the silk thread unites the pearls of a necklace — nature's inflexible law which encircles the globe with a ribbon of delicate and irreplaceable gems.

Islands are small worlds unto themselves. Many of them have existed for a very long time and have witnessed the evolution of unique animal and vegetal species. The particular climatic conditions, the diversity of geological origins, the absence of large predators which need wide open spaces to develop, have created a myriad of indigenous laboratories and multiplied the opportunities for life. Needing to adapt themselves to a special environment, insular fauna and flora have developed a systematic particularization transforming their mini-habitat into a unique and therefore priceless microcosm. Distance converted the islands into biological combat areas which have expanded considerably the scope of our genetic inheritance. We must protect this sacred trust, remembering that nothing is more precious than life.

In 1963, on board the *Calypso* anchored in the shelter of the Cape Verde Islands, I contemplated with sadness the land's barren profile where the odd thorny bush struggled to grow on heat-cracked stones. What happened to the mighty forests, the great rivers and the fertile land the first explorers found? Memories of some old lectures came to mind: Plato describing the thoughtless felling of Crete's broad-leaved trees to construct boats and build houses . . . The great dead and sightless statues on Easter Island. Islands mistreated by man have been granted no mercy. The narrowness of their confines, the insidious corrosion of the salt air, the uncontrolled wearing of erosion preclude any healing reprieve. Once begun, the destruction of the fragile ecological equilibrium cannot be halted. The laborious products of an unremitting process are destroyed in a mere few years, and the penalty is always the same: death. Only a few fossils will remain and bear witness some day to the fact that this oasis of life was devastated by man's voraciousness and has been turned by him into a tomb.

Today, we cannot be excused on the same grounds as our ancestors who were driven by hun-

The giant Pacific octopus has the remarkable ability to change the colour and even the texture of its skin. Red colouration usually accompanies territorial aggression or sexual arousal.

ger, stimulated by an insatiable curiosity and protected by their ignorance. We know that nature must be protected rather than attacked. An imperative moral task orders us — temporary occupants of the planet life — to transmit our heritage in as good a condition as possible to our successors. All living species are our legitimate fellow-tenants. We do not have the right to evict anyone, to consider any species as unimportant and even less to write any species off on a bookkeeper's profit and loss ledger. Our wisdom tells us that we still have much to learn, even from the most modest of cells. Our conscience forbids us to be destructive since we have finally understood that a superior moral order takes precedence over economic considerations.

I still do not know the Queen Charlotte archipelago, but I place myself wholeheartedly among its defenders. We are in the same camp. Planet and life are one, and our mother, the Earth, cries out to us: the harm that you have inflicted upon the humblest of my islands, it is upon me, the whole Earth, that you have inflicted it.

Jacques Cousteau

Clouds, Cape Freeman, Moresby Island, 1981—Toni Onley

INTRODUCTION

One hundred kilometres out from the mainland coast of British Columbia, perched on the very edge of Canada's Pacific continental shelf, lie the Queen Charlotte Islands. Their shores bathed in the nutrient-rich waters of the north Pacific Ocean and their climate tempered by warmer offshore currents, they are blessed with abundant natural resources of sea and forest. A refuge from the full impact of the last great ice age, they support an ancient and unique community of plant and animal life. They are also the home of the Haida who, within this tremendously wealthy natural environment, developed one of the world's outstanding aboriginal cultures.

Like most of the earth's prolific places, the Charlottes have a powerful spirit about them, an essential quality that permeates everything and lends its vibration to the distinctive characteristics of the region. It shows in ten thousand elusive ways, from the peculiar shapes of landforms to the manner of a simple leaf unfolding. You can smell it in the air, hear it in the limbs of the trees, and feel it moving in the earth beneath your feet. You can find it in the stories, speech, songs, politics and art of the people who live there — and the longer people live in the place, the deeper they become enmeshed in its web of life, and the more pronounced and articulated that special quality becomes in their culture.

There is an old Haida story about a character called Stoneribs, who appeared unremarkable as a child until the day he lowered himself into a stone bathtub. Bracing his arms and legs against the sides, he pushed with all his might . . . and shattered the tub. Another was brought to him and again he pressed against its sides until it broke. After he had burst four stone tubs he acquired supernatural powers, went out and killed the fearsome five-finned killer-whale, and did many good deeds for his people.

This story contains a hint of that essential quality of the Charlottes — a combination of tension, expectancy and compression. There is a great energy bound up in the very shapes of things, ready to burst out with a crack like a four-inch plank splitting off a massive cedar log. It's a feeling that sooner or later something has to give, and in fact it often does: the Charlottes are the most earthquake-active area in North America.

It's in the air too, most noticeably when the great north Pacific low-pressure system moves in and broods over the islands. The sky turns grey as slate and feels just as heavy. The sea flattens to glass, the horizon blurs in mist and rain. The firmament shrinks around you. Your mind pushes out against it, searching for a horizon, probing for something familiar to get the measure of things. Again, something has to give, and again it usually does, erupting into gales that blow for days like trade winds, often building during the larger tides into storm force winds of 160 kilometres an hour or more. The Charlottes have the highest average annual wind speed in Canada.

But nowhere is this quality of tension and compression more apparent than in Haida art, the form of expression and celebration of the people immersed for so long in the natural-spiritual mosaic of the Charlottes. Flat surfaces are decorated with complex and powerful graphic images, constructed

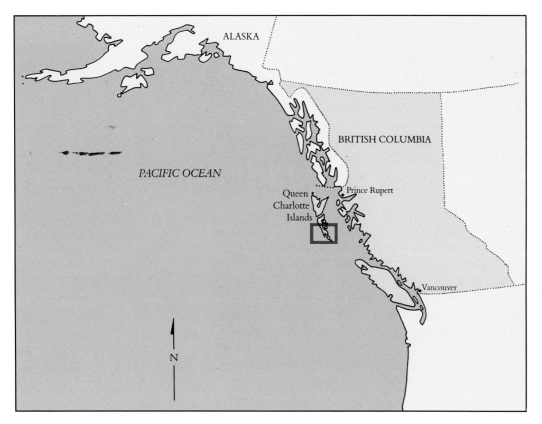

Perched on the edge of the continental shelf, the Queen Charlotte archipelago (above) is the most isolated land mass in Canada. The red line (opposite) indicates the northern boundary of the South Moresby Wilderness Proposal drawn in 1974.

from variations on a fundamental abstract form: the ovoid. This dynamic wedding of the rectangle and the oval swells and tapers and winds its way through the graphic field with remarkable tension, bending just to the point where it appears ready to snap — but never beyond. Nor is the tension ever relieved. The three-dimensional carved figures on bowls, spoons and ceremonial poles are composed of the same basic elements, except that the planes they occupy have been wrapped, bent and twisted into shapes so fair to the eye and so lively in spite of their abstraction that the creatures they portray seem al-

ways about to leap out and begin to dance before your eyes.

At the southern end of the Queen Charlotte archipelago is an area called South Moresby which even local residents, accustomed as they are to living with excessive natural beauty, have long considered a special place. A naturalist's dream, it stretches from the abyssal depths of the Pacific Ocean to the peaks of the San Cristoval mountains — the rugged backbone of South Moresby — some one thousand metres above sea level. It encompasses 138 islands of all shapes and sizes and 42 freshwater lakes. The west coast is exposed to the thundering surf and awesome storms of the open Pacific and has been called the highest energy coastline in Canada. On the more sheltered east coast, quiet fiords, bays, lagoons, tidal estuaries, sandy beaches, sea caves and offshore reefs combine to form the living fabric of a Pacific wilderness. In fact it is a microcosm of the whole Canadian Pacific coast, the mainland in miniature.

Flowering plants, some unique in the world, flourish in high alpine gardens. At lower elevations a virgin rainforest forms a green mantle over the landscape, much as it has for more than ten thousand years. Thriving in the cool, moist maritime climate are giant red cedars, Sitka spruce, western hemlock and yellow cypress, ranking with the largest trees remaining on earth. These monarchs were already centuries old when Columbus arrived in the Western Hemisphere.

More than sixteen hundred kilometres of coastal shoreline provide habitat for a tremendous diversity of marine intertidal life. Whales, porpoises, seals and over one-half of British Columbia's sea lion population thrive in its plankton-rich waters. The

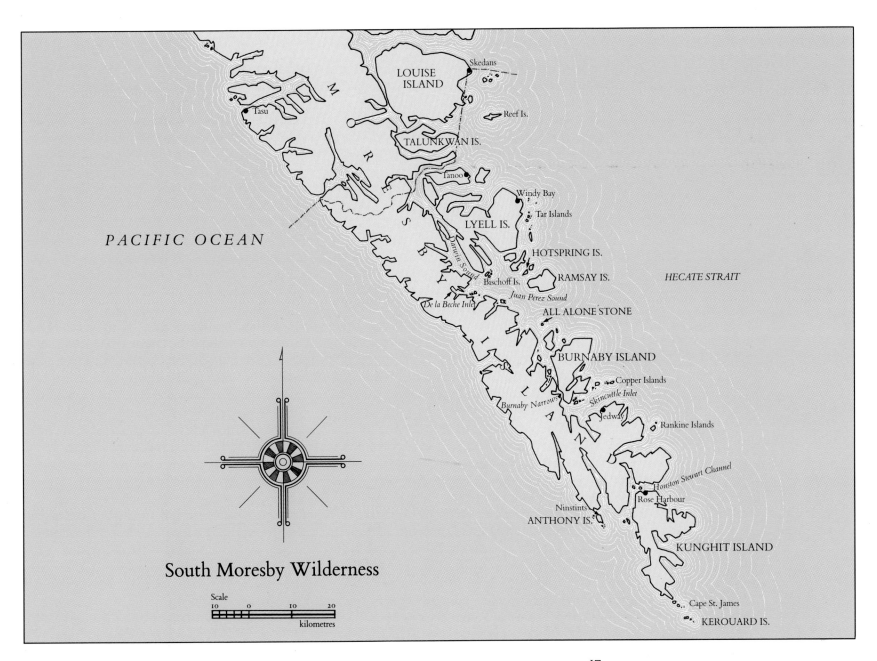

PACIFIC OCEAN

LOUISE ISLAND

Skedans

Tasu

Reef Is.

TALUNKWAN IS.

Tanoo

Windy Bay

Tar Islands

LYELL IS.

HOTSPRING IS.

HECATE STRAIT

Bischoff Is.

RAMSAY IS.

De la Beche Inlet

Juan Perez Sound

ALL ALONE STONE

BURNABY ISLAND

Copper Islands

Burnaby Narrows

Skincuttle Inlet

Jedway

Rankine Islands

Houston Stewart Channel

Rose Harbour

Ninstints

ANTHONY IS.

KUNGHIT ISLAND

South Moresby Wilderness

Scale

10   0   10   20

kilometres

Cape St. James

KEROUARD IS.

area supports over 25 percent of all the nesting seabirds on the Canadian Pacific — one quarter of a million breeding pairs. Preying upon this abundant food source are Peale's peregrine falcons, spectacular raptors which survive here in the world's greatest concentrations. Bald eagles nest in South Moresby in densities unparalleled anywhere else in Canada. The area is a major stopover for migrating waterfowl along the Pacific flyway. Trumpeter swans and sandhill cranes are among the endangered species which find refuge in this isolated corner of the earth.

The world's largest black bear and a unique pine marten with orange under-fur are among the seven land mammals found in South Moresby that show evolutionary distinctions from those on the mainland. These and other endemic species have resulted in the Queen Charlottes being called the "Canadian Galapagos," a natural history laboratory for scientific study.

South Moresby is also the territory of Raven, Foam Woman, Killer Whale, Sacred-One-Both-Standing-Still-And-Moving, Stoneribs and a host of other powerful supernatural beings who feature in the cultural achievements of the Haida. Today some four hundred Haida archaeological sites are found here, including the world's largest array of totem poles still standing in their natural setting at Ninstints on Anthony Island, now protected as a UNESCO World Heritage Cultural Site. These monuments in cedar evoke powerful images of the great culture that flourished here for thousands of years.

In November 1974, a logging company filed for permission to begin harvesting operations in the heart of South Moresby. The proposal sparked a movement to save the area which has grown over the past decade into one of Canada's foremost wilderness conservation issues.

Opposition to the logging plans began with the Skidegate Band Council, whose members hold strong ancestral ties to South Moresby and still depend upon the area for food and spiritual sustenance. They were joined by the Islands Protection Society (IPS), which formed to voice the general public's environmental concerns for the area. A proposal to create a South Moresby Wilderness Area was submitted to the government of British Columbia, resulting in the deferral of logging plans and a decade of scientific study, political controversy, and discovery of South Moresby by a growing number of wilderness recreationists.

As of the date of this writing, the Council of the Haida Nation has registered a claim of aboriginal title over the whole of the Queen Charlottes which has not been settled. The Environment and Land Use Committee of the Provincial Cabinet has collected much of the scientific information into a technical report called *South Moresby, Land Use Alternatives,* and its members have announced their intention to visit the area before deciding its fate.

The results of the past ten years of exploration — the scientific studies, the photographs by a great many amateur and professional photographers, and the paintings and prints of artists — taken all together form a wealth of information about South Moresby. Today, on the eve of the decision, we have chosen to publish this selection of some of the work which has helped shape our awareness of South Moresby's special values.

The book opens with an examination by Bill Reid of our age-old penchant for "going forth and subduing" the earth. Drawing on the allegorical traditions of his German father and Haida mother (from the village of Tanoo in South Moresby), he describes the swath cut by history through the wild places and aboriginal cultures of the earth, right up to the edges of the last few remaining places in the world that have not yet been transformed.

The second section is an anthology of four natural history essays. Dr. J. Bristol Foster portrays the special features of the evolutionary process peculiar to the Queen Charlotte Islands, and describes their unique mammals, plants, birds, fish and insects. Dr. Jim Pojar and John Broadhead describe South Moresby's terrestrial ecosystems from the high alpine parkland to the ancient coastal rainforest, world-famous for its huge specimens of spruce, hemlock and cedar, and its primeval mix of plant species. David Denning explores the marine environment of South Moresby, the underwater paradise which is home to an awesome display of vertebrate and invertebrate marine life forms. Lastly, Wayne Campbell explains the nutrient cycles of the northeastern Pacific basin and the phenomenal seabird and raptor populations which have developed as an integral part of them.

The third and last part consists of two chapters which describe the issues that have made South Moresby one of B.C.'s most complex and celebrated wilderness conservation issues. John Broadhead de-

scribes the events which have transformed this grassroots conservation issue into an international ground swell of popular support. Delving into the politics of resource use in British Columbia, he calls for a thoughtful examination and change in our attitude towards the land that sustains us. Finally, Thom Henley addresses the hazard of popularizing a wilderness area for the purpose of saving it: the possibility of attracting far more people than fragile wilderness values are capable of tolerating.

An industrial tree farm deals in tree production, a so-called renewable resource. Fragile wilderness values are not renewable, at least not for half a millenium or so, provided that the necessary parent species needed for recovery have not been obliterated by the process of industrial extraction. A decision is about to be made by a handful of elected officials, in office for only a few years, which could result in the loss for a great many years of values in South Moresby cherished by many people. Yet the land and the trees are after all publicly owned, if not by the native Haida or the citizens of British Columbia, then by the whole of the planet. So it is important that we be as well informed as possible about what is at stake, and that we focus keen attention on the decision-making process. It is in this spirit that this book is offered.

John Broadhead and Thom Henley, directors — IPS

Spirits of the Forest—Hermit Thrush, 1982—Robert Bateman

PART I

THE LEGACY OF CHANGE

THESE SHINING ISLANDS

A few thousand years ago, a mere tick of the cosmic clock, but quite a respectable time when measured by the rapid pace of a people intent on overtaking their own destiny as soon as possible, the god of a then-obscure tribe came up with a rather questionable dictate:

"Be fruitful and multiply and replenish the earth and subdue it."

Fruitful they were, multiplying mightily and industriously subduing as they did so — converting forests into pasture, pasture into desert and all that. In due course they were subdued themselves, but that grand old command was far too useful to discard. It suited the inclinations of the victors just as well as it had the vanquished. And when, about four hundred years ago, it was rendered into its finest form, expressed in the resonant English of the King James version — powerful, poetic, unequivocally

on the side of the strong and aggressive — the great going forth and, most dramatically, subduing, was approaching full momentum.

The local warlords had begun the process by subduing their immediate neighbours, and later those not so immediate, and so created countries and empires which tried to subdue each other and sometimes succeeded. They certainly subdued the countryside — first of all cutting down the trees to build cities, palaces, churches . . . and navies.

Some of the ships of these navies, of the few to survive the constant bloody neighbourhood quarrels which were a more or less constant part of life in those and later times, set out to discover what lay beyond the reaches of the known seas. They were sailed by men so foolhardy or courageous, so adventurous or avaricious — take your choice — and so convinced of their own abilities and purpose, that

South Moresby, with Hecate Strait in the foreground and the Pacific Ocean beyond.

23

their exploits are still a source of wonder and admiration, regardless of their methods and motivations.

Everywhere they went they found traces of that old garden from which they had been banished long ago. Well, the purpose of all this going forth certainly wasn't to go back to anything, and they proceeded to change these demi-paradises into something they could deal with, usually starting by cutting down the trees.

Sometimes they found great cities, the homes of people with cultures as advanced as their own, and sometimes so beautiful they thought they had stumbled into fairyland, so they promptly destroyed them. Sometimes they found beautiful, gentle, generous people, so they made slaves of them and killed them.

Sometimes they found people who weren't so nice, or beautiful, or gentle or generous, but were almost as avaricious and acquisitive as they were themselves. These they dealt with as allies or trading partners until they'd relieved them of the goods they coveted; then they destroyed them and their cultures.

Of course, at the same time mankind was up to many other things, not all of them so bad. Man, at least a few men, largely through the exploitation of the new wealth from beyond the seas, gained the time and the technology to learn more of the universe and themselves. They developed artists who looked at the world with fresh eyes and found that the parts of it not yet touched by all this subduing were perhaps the most beautiful, and that even human beings could be beautiful. The writers and philosophers began to wonder if they also might

have the capacity to be good and kind, generous and gentle. It even occurred to them that their old god, whose first instructions they had been obeying so assiduously, might have meant some of the other things he had said about enemies, neighbours, children and fellow humans in general.

Unfortunately he never got around to the creatures great and small with whom we share the earth, and the land on which we live.

The poets, who'd had such a good time for so long telling of great subduings of this and that, began to sing of peaceful seas and tigers burning bright, of little lambs and other wonders of the non-human world. Some people at least came to suspect that the world may have some kind of function other than to be consumed as rapidly as possible for their immediate gratification. They even began to realize that killing all those great and small creatures — either to eat or wear or just for fun, or because they took up some of the room or ate some of the food they wanted for themselves — was neither the most profitable nor the most intelligent way of dealing with them, and might not have been the destiny their god had in mind when he created them.

The realization came too late to do most of the wild animals much good. The wolves had long since gone from Wales and the rest of Europe, along with most of the other wild creatures. What the subduers had done at home, they accomplished with equal efficiency as they made their way around the world.

That tiger who once transformed the night's arboreal gloom with his bright shining now dimly glows in zoos and roadside tourist traps.

The great herds of Africa are gone, their surviving numbers eroded by the pressure of poachers and

the harvesting considered necessary to prevent the overpopulation of their steadily shrinking preserves.

In North America, they once told of a hypothetical squirrel who could have made his way from the shores of the Atlantic Ocean to the banks of Mississippi River, leaping from branch to branch through the forest without ever touching the ground. They spoke of flocks of birds so dense they obscured the sun with their passing, of rivers and lakes alive with fish, and of unbelievably huge herds of bison, deer and pronghorn antelope that swept across the great central plains.

Well, the rivers, lakes, shores and ocean depths no longer exactly teem with fish. And, although they have shown an almost unbelievable stubbornness in persisting to survive the guns, traps, snares and ravaged habitats which face them everywhere, the birds are only a remnant of what they once were. Today you can travel coast to coast and if you're lucky you may see a few deer or a half-dozen pronghorns. But it's much more likely that the only living animals you'll see are some domestic horses and cattle, seemingly rooted in a geometric landscape.

Even Leviathan, the mightiest creature who ever lived, has almost been swept from myth and history. So few are his numbers that he must call halfway around the world to find another of his own kind with whom to keep his incredible lineage alive. Even this desperate voyage in search of survival too often ends short of its goal, in the sickening blast that tears through the long, smooth muscles, designed to propel him effortlessly around the globe — the only living being whose passage matches the mighty surge of the ocean itself.

Almost every place in the world — from the tropical rain forests to the Antarctic, from Lake Baikal to Lake Superior — the effects of the tremendous crushing, consuming, destroying, transforming thrust of energy either have or soon will be felt. It is a wave that started on the smallest continent and spread outwards around the sphere of the planet until it has eventually, inevitably, closed in upon itself. Today the wave reverberates in small, scattered centres of turbulence, lashing with undiminished avarice at the few isolated enclaves it has yet to consume.

One of these is South Moresby in the Queen Charlotte Islands.

For thousands of years the Charlottes lay secure in their isolation, protected by the sea even from the ice that swept south to cover most of the continent. Because of this isolation these islands gave birth to many unusual, in some cases unique, kinds of animal and plant life. And when about ten thousand years ago some newcomers penetrated their isolation, arriving by sea or being coaxed out of a clamshell by Raven, they too were transformed into a people as unusual and in some ways as unique as their environment — the Haida.

Among their accomplishments were the great Northwest coast canoes, each ingeniously fashioned from a single cedar tree and ranging in length up to twenty-one metres, as beautiful as any of the wonderful vessels maritime man has ever devised. Possessing the skills needed to build these graceful seagoing boats and with a wonderful sense of design, they filled their lives with one of the most elegant and refined material cultures in the tribal world. They found room for expression on a myriad of objects, ranging from the world famous totem poles and the beautifully proportioned houses they complemented, to exquisite items of personal adorn-

Even Leviathan, the mightiest creature who ever lived, has almost been swept from myth and history. Opposite: breaching humpback whale, west coast of Moresby Island.

27

The Haida as they once were are part of history now. (Skidegate, 1878)

their land. The properties of the great families have been claimed and parts have been changed, perhaps forever, by the great subduers . . . remember them? They've been up to their old practices here as elsewhere, destroying peoples and cultures and cutting down the trees, so that now only a few isolated areas remain untouched.

One of these is South Moresby, and fortunately for us it is one of the richest and most desirable parts of the Queen Charlottes. In the opinion of many people who know these islands well, if they had to make a choice to conserve just one area of the Charlottes as they were when only the Haida lived there, they would choose South Moresby.

Why? First because of its overwhelming beauty — hundreds of islands, each with a character as distinctive as its name: Hotspring, All Alone Stone, Flowerpot, Tuft, Flatrock, Monument, and many more. And these are just our prosaic English names. The old Haida had much more expressive ways of identifying their intimate environment, such as *Killer-Whale-With-Two-Heads, Sunshine-Upon-His-Breast* and *Red-Cod-Island*.

Then there's the sea and shore life, fish so numerous that one need never spend more than a few minutes in quest of something delicious for the next meal, shellfish in profusion: one narrow channel about a kilometre long, Burnaby Narrows, is reputed to contain more protein per square metre of bottom than any other place in the world. Not to mention the birds and mammals of land and sea, an abundance and diversity of life unrivalled on the coast.

And towering above it all, both physically and symbolically, is the forest. Here are the great cedars from which the Haida constructed their material

ment, all relating to the complex genealogical patterns which gave structure to their lives. The heraldic art which they developed stands alone among the arts of the world in its concept of the formline, one of the most intellectually refined and aesthetically powerful systems of expression, a feat of the imagination that truly deserves to be called unique.

Well, the Haida as they once were are part of history now. A small remnant of their never very numerous population still tenaciously clings to their identity and to some fragments of their culture and

28

Bear mortuary pole at Ninstints on Skun gwai. *(Red Cod Island)*

Creating the myths of a living culture. (Dogfish pole by Bill Reid, Skidegate, 1978)

culture, and incredibly huge spruce and hemlock and a thousand other kinds of plants spread upon the forest floor and clinging to the limbs of trees. In short, it is an unmistakable part of that old garden, and because it is one of the few pieces remaining, it is incalculably valuable. Not in terms of the subduers' cash flow and balance sheets, or even in the more human context of jobs and wages. There is no dollar-and-cents equivalent with which to measure the sacred.

It may be that few people will ever find their way to visit these remote shores, although they do offer one of the rare remaining opportunities to witness such a profusion of life in such a concentrated area. When, or if, we should ever decide that subduing is not the only, or even the most desirable, way of making our way through the world, these shining islands may be the signposts that point the way to a renewed harmonious relationship with this, the only world we're ever going to have.

Perhaps saving them is a promise and a hope, a being conscious of their continued existence whether we as individuals ever actually see them or not, so that we may return to a more peaceable kingdom with a full knowledge of its wonders. Without South Moresby and the other places like it, we may forget what we once were and what we can be again, and lose our humanity in a world devoid of the amazing non-humans with whom we have shared it.

I have four grandchildren, three of them growing up in the village of Skidegate on the Queen Charlottes, the fourth a frequent visitor. I would like to think that as they become the Haida of the future, the people who call these beautiful, bountiful islands their home, they and their peers will have more than nostalgic, regretful memories of "how it used to be in the old days" upon which to build their own visions of their past. I would like to know that they can go to at least one sacred place that has not been crushed by the juggernaut of the subduers and there create the myths of a living culture. There is nowhere more worthy of the care and reverence due the sacred places of the earth than this.

These shining islands may be the signposts that point the way to a renewed harmonious relationship with this, the only world we're ever going to have. (Burnaby Narrows)

Fisherman's Patience—Peale Inlet, West Coast, 1982—Donald Curley

PART II

THE NATURAL HISTORY

THE CANADIAN GALAPAGOS

A remote archipelago eight hundred kilometres off the west coast of South America — the Galapagos Islands — has captured the entire world's interest for the unique biological forms found there. Yet few people are aware that only one hundred kilometres from British Columbia's west coast lies a group of islands scientists call the Canadian Galapagos — the Queen Charlotte Islands — which are themselves an evolutionary showcase.

Like that more famous archipelago to the south, they harbour an astonishing array of unusual plants and animals. In fact, considering the size of the islands, there are more endemic (peculiar to one place) and disjunct (widely separated) kinds of plants and animals here than in any other area of Canada. What is it about islands, and in particular about the Charlottes, that causes such biological anomalies?

The question is difficult to answer, for during the last tens of thousands of years the evolutionary process has gone on virtually unrecorded. But evolution has left hints, and scientists acting as detectives can offer us carefully thought-out and well-supported theories to help us imagine how these islands came to be the way they are today.

Charles Darwin put the Galapagos Islands on the map — and his name on the roster of the famous — when he noted that each of the islands seemed to be home to similar yet distinctly different kinds of finches. In 1859 he wrote: "Seeing this gradation and diversity of structure in one small, intimately related group of birds, one might really fancy that from an original paucity of birds in this archipelago, one species had been taken and modified for different ends." His conclusion, that species were not after all immutable, but changing — evolving, in

The isolation of the Queen Charlotte Islands has made them a showcase of evolution. Opposite: view from the San Cristoval Range, Moresby Island.

35

fact — flew directly in the face of contemporary belief, and its implication is still rocking today's theological community.

Not only is life on earth constantly evolving, but the earth itself — rock and sand, water and air — is also in continual flux. Geologists, studying the earth's surface, have developed a theory called "plate tectonics" according to which the earth's crust, a layer of rock several kilometres thick, is cracked into massive, constantly moving segments called plates. Each plate moves separately, sometimes colliding with one another and forming mountains, sometimes overriding one another.

Along the western edge of North America, about 120 million years ago, a massive tectonic change began. In response to intense geological pressures, the Farallon Plate underlying the northeast section of the Pacific Ocean began to slide inexorably beneath the continent. The edge of the continental plate buckled and heaved upwards, breaking off blocks of the earth's crust. Over millions of years this cast-off rubble eventually drifted into the northeast corner of the Pacific basin and coalesced into what we now call the Queen Charlotte Islands.

The legacy of stresses which must have accompanied all of this crustal movement is with us still. There are more earthquakes in the Queen Charlotte area than anywhere else in Canada. The Farallon Plate is still sliding under the continental plate very near the west coast of the Charlottes, moving at about the same pace as a fingernail grows. In places the fault line is only a few kilometres offshore. From there the ocean floor drops off abruptly to over three thousand metres.

Because the formation of new species is usually dependent on isolation, islands such as the Queen Charlottes or the Galapagos are natural laboratories for studying evolution. As long as no new genetic information is bred into a particular population, a toad or bird or flowering plant will respond to local conditions by evolving body structures or life strategies often quite different from its distant relatives.

It is not surprising then that the isolated Charlottes have become an evolutionary showcase. But around this very issue of remoteness a controversy has sprung up between the theories of two branches of science.

Geologists tell us that as recently as ten thousand years ago British Columbia was covered by the glaciers of the last great ice age. Some claim that the ice sheet entirely covered the Queen Charlottes. But biologists insist that the biological peculiarities found on the islands today must have taken more than ten thousand years to evolve. How could that evolution have occurred if the land was buried under a massive sheet of ice?

To deal with this quandary, scientists have postulated another theory, one which is supported by decades of research. It states that on these islands were ice-free pockets, called refugia, in which plant and animal families survived while masses of ice scraped the surrounding landscape down to bedrock.

The lack of a continental shelf off the Charlottes' west coast may have been the reason why refugia existed among the glaciers of the last ice epoch. Without the shelf, it may have been impossible for snow to pile up sufficiently to form glaciers. More likely the snow would have avalanched into the ocean, leaving possible footholds for hardy plants and animals to survive the winters and live a productive, albeit sparse, life cycle in the summers.

We do not know for sure which of the plants and

Ten thousand years ago the Queen Charlottes may have looked much like this view of the St. Elias Range in Alaska. Even if totally glaciated, it is still possible for hardy life forms to survive on nunataks — ice-free summits.

37

Evidence of glacial refugia on the Charlottes comes from many quarters. Grains of pollen trapped in the muck in bogs for over eleven thousand years tell the story of a mature, stabilized forest living at a time when the rest of British Columbia was buried under ice.

animals now found on the Charlottes arrived first. We do know, however, that most unique forms of the native land mammals (deer mouse, black bear, pine marten, ermine, dusky shrew, caribou), the saw-whet owl, Steller's jay and hairy woodpecker, certain insects, amphipods, stickleback fish, mosses, liverworts and several flowering plants live only on the Charlottes and *nowhere else in the world*. There are also several plant species whose nearest relatives are scattered around the planet but do not occur anywhere else in the new world.

The biological support for the refugia theory comes from many quarters. For example, bogs tend to trap and preserve grains of pollen, one of the most durable organic forms known, for thousands of years. Scientists can determine what species of plant a particular pollen grain came from and how long ago it was deposited. Several bogs on the Charlottes were investigated by palaeobotanist C. S. Heusser in the late 1950s.

On Langara Island, Heusser found the oldest record of life among any of the bog borings yet made in British Columbia and southeastern Alaska. At the bottom of almost seven metres of muck in one bog he discovered eleven-thousand-year-old pollen, which would place it geologically at about the same time as the continental ice sheet was retreating from the Charlottes. The curious thing about these pollen grains in this ancient bog is that they tell the story of a mature, stabilized forest, one which had developed a complex variety of species. This is hardly the sort of colony one would expect to find immediately after the retreat of a blanket of ice.

Recently, on the exposed sandy bluffs near Cape Ball along the eastern shore of Graham Island, palaeobotanist Rolf Matthewes and associates discovered some fascinating new evidence of the way things were during glaciation. Although the bluffs are only 4.5 metres high, they provide a continuous record of environmental changes since the last ice age. Radiocarbon datings taken from fossilized plant fragments and pollen indicate that about sixteen thousand years ago, while the rest of British Columbia was heavily glaciated, this region was free of ice. Once again scientists found evidence of an abundance of species where there should have been none.

The best examples of plants that have survived glaciation are found among the mosses and liverworts. These tiny, non-flowering plants cover most of the ground and branches of trees in coastal British Columbia. Dr. W. B. Schofield, a botanist at the University of British Columbia, has been particularly energetic in tracing their relationships on the Charlottes, the moss capital of the world.

Schofield has found species of moss that exist only on the Charlottes: *Wijkia carlottae* (distantly related to a Himalayan species), *Seligeria careyana*, two new species of sphagnum moss and one species of *Bazzania,* or liverwort.

Even more intriguing are the disjunct species that occur only on the Charlottes and in distant places. For example, the moss *Dichodontium subporodictyon* is found solely on the Charlottes, in the Himalayas and in Scotland. *Mastopoma haidensis* occurs on the Charlottes and on the Brooks Peninsula of Vancouver Island, with one distant relative in Borneo. *Gollania turgens* occurs only on the Charlottes and in glacial refugia in Alaska, the Yukon and China. *Zygodon gracilis* lives on the Charlottes and in Britain, *Daltonia splachnoides* on the Charlottes and Southern Ireland, *Wijkia hornbschuchii* on the Charlottes and in Southeast Asia.

The Queen Charlotte Islands have been called the "moss capital of the world" because they harbour an exceptional number of mosses and liverworts. Some of these exist only on the Charlottes; others are paired with plants in widely disjunct locations such as Bhutan, western Ireland or Borneo.

High on the mist-shrouded slopes of the San Cristoval Range, Senecio newcombei *grows in profusion. One of the four flowering plants unique to the Charlottes, it reinforces the refugium theory and illustrates a characteristic of island evolution — the survival of ancient lifeforms now extinct on the mainland.*

The liverworts follow the same pattern: *Dendrobazzania griffithiana* is found only on the Charlottes and in Bhutan, north of India; *Herbertus sendtnera* in the Charlottes, the Alps and the Himalayas; *Mastigophora woodsii* in the Charlottes, Britain, the Faroe Islands and the Himalayas; *Chandonanthus hirtellus* in the Charlottes, Japan and Australasia; *Anastrophyllum donianum* in the Charlottes, oceanic Europe and the Faroe Islands; *Scapania ornithopodioides* in the Charlottes, alpine Japan, the Himalayas and Britain.

Flowering plants on the Charlottes also hold some surprises. *Senecio newcombei,* a small yellow flowering plant, is unique to the Charlottes. It is only distantly related to a species in Oregon and Colorado. Until recently it was thought that about ten more species were unique, until they were also found on the Brooks Peninsula of northwestern Vancouver Island. Possibly the Brooks Peninsula was also a refugium during the last ice age.

There are four other kinds of flowering plants that are unique to the Charlottes: saxifrage (*Saxifraga punctata,* ssp *carlottae*), alpine lily (*Lloydia serotina,* ssp *flava*), willow (*Salix reticulata,* ssp *glabellicarpa*) and monkey flower (*Mimulus guttatus,* ssp *haidensis*).

These plants which exist on the Charlottes and perhaps in a few other places scattered around the world reinforce the refugia theory. If the liverwort *Dendrobazzania griffithiana* is found only on the Charlottes and in Bhutan, it must at one time have existed eastward from Bhutan, across Asia and the land bridge to Alaska. From there its range must have extended at least as far south as the Queen Charlottes, perhaps via a land bridge from the mainland to what is now the Queen Charlotte Islands.

Then, when massive icefields intruded, covering much of the northern hemisphere, *Dendrobazzania griffithiana* must have survived in refugia in Bhutan and the Queen Charlotte Islands. The Queen Charlotte refugia theory is reinforced further by the very number of disjunct life forms found there.

But what about animals?

A sea flea or amphipod, *Paramoera carlottensis,* unique to the Charlottes, lives in brackish tidepools. It is easy to imagine this creature surviving the ice age, for the ocean to the west of the Charlottes would not have been frozen. Likewise, some of the endemic kinds of flightless beetles and a spittle bug could probably have survived in a small refugium without major difficulties.

But the warm-blooded animals are another matter. Birds do not hibernate, and of the endemic mammals on the Charlottes, only the black bear becomes torpid. The others would have had to put up with long periods of cold and heavy snowfall.

One might expect the endemic birds to be arctic-adapted like the ptarmigan. However, the three endemic birds — owl, woodpecker and jay — prefer deep forest. They are rarely found in the subalpine, a sparse and rugged ecosystem similar to what the refugia on the islands might have been like.

Only three of the endemic mammals — the ermine, bear and caribou — seem well adapted to wintery conditions. And yet shrews, deer mice, marten and river otter all live under arctic conditions today. All obviously could have survived in a refugium.

The small mammals and stickleback fish of the Charlottes, being easily captured in large numbers, have been thoroughly studied. Great variation has been found within the species. It is almost possible

Just as Charles Darwin found a different finch or tortoise on each of the Galapagos Islands, so it is possible on the Charlottes to find a different kind of deer mouse on each island or a different stickleback (above) in each lake. The range of unique kinds of fish, plants, birds, mammals and insects on these islands is greater than any other place in Canada and includes (opposite, clockwise from upper left): hairy woodpecker, Saxifrage taylori, *Steller's jay,* Senecio newcombei, *saw-whet owl and dusky shrew.*

to describe a different kind of deer mouse from each island, a different stickleback from each lake.

Obviously, the isolation of the Charlottes has prevented interbreeding with mainland plants and animals. Moreover, the movement of mice between islands or stickleback fish between lakes has probably been minimal. Add to this the lack of glaciation on parts of the Charlottes and we are left with the likelihood that we are dealing with exceptionally old life forms in some cases, not simply newcomers since glaciation.

There are five characteristics of life on islands which help account for the unique kinds of animals found here:

1. Islands always have fewer species than the nearby mainland. The Charlottes has the Steller's jay, saw-whet owl, hairy woodpecker, blue grouse, pine grosbeak but lacks the gray jay, screech owl, downy woodpecker, ruffed grouse and evening grosbeak present on the adjacent mainland. There are native black bears but no grizzly, marten but no fisher, deer mice but no voles, chipmunks or native squirrels. There are ermine on the islands but no least weasels. There were caribou but no native deer, goats or sheep.

2. Those animals that do reach an island always have fewer predators and competitors. This fact can alter the whole basis for their survival. The selective forces are different, as will be the animals themselves after enough generations.

3. The more isolated the island, the fewer the number of species that will be present there. This accounts for the relatively few kinds of life on the Charlottes, which are the most isolated islands in Canada.

4. The smaller the island, the fewer the number of species. Within the Charlottes, black bear, marten and ermine are not found on the smaller islands.

5. Mainland forms tend to displace island forms when they manage to get to an island (Seton's Law). This is because mainland forms tend to be more efficient than relatives on islands.

Given these characteristics, as well as the special features of the Charlottes' isolation and the glaciation described earlier, the native Charlotte land mammals come into perspective more clearly.

Dawson caribou *(Rangifer dawsoni),* the most intriguing of the island mammals, apparently went extinct several decades ago. It was a very distinctive caribou, much smaller than the mainland variety, proving that species of deer tend to become smaller when confined to islands.

Since the glaciers melted and the dense forest spread, caribou habitat has steadily declined. Perhaps the Dawson caribou was already close to extinction by the time the black-tailed deer was introduced early in the century. This efficient browser could well have pushed the caribou to extinction, as predicted by Seton's Law.

The Haida ermine *(Mustela erminea haidarum)* is very uncommon and is particularly distinctive compared to mainland weasels. It has many characteristics similar to arctic weasels, suggesting that it survived glaciation in the Charlotte refugia. Exactly why this ermine is so rare remains a mystery, for mice and birds seem to supply plenty of food and there are fewer predators and similar-sized competitors than on the nearby mainland.

The pine marten *(Martes americana nesophila)* is fairly common on the Charlottes today and can

The end of a species—the last two Dawson caribou (photographed in 1908). Animals isolated on islands often tend to be either dwarfs or giants compared to their mainland relatives. The Dawson caribou is an example of a species that evolved into a smaller version of itself, whereas the Queen Charlotte's endemic black bear is the world's largest.

more from adjacent bears in Alaska, mainland B.C. and Vancouver Island than any of them differ from each other. Indeed, the Charlotte black bear is unusual, and its characteristics could have developed during a long period of glaciation. Its diet then, as today, likely would have been large quantities of intertidal crabs captured by turning over rocks. This nutritious but highly abrasive food might account for the bear's particularly large teeth.

Dusky shrews *(Sorex obscurus)* are represented by two varieties on the Charlottes. One of these, *elassodon* differs markedly from nearby mainland shrews and therefore perhaps survived in the refugia for thousands of years. The other, *prevostensis,* is similar to other shrews and is perhaps a relatively recent arrival.

Deer mice *(Peromyscus)* have been studied intensely since they are easily trapped in large numbers. While these mice could have existed in the refugia on the Charlottes, a simpler theory is that a small deer mouse reached the Charlottes at the close of glaciation. Eventually mice could have reached most of the islands by way of land bridges, log rafts, Indian canoes and so on.

The main reasons the Charlottes are so special — unique plants and animals and a rich Haida cultural heritage — are the result of their isolation. The introduction of regular ferry service to the islands, begun in 1981 by the B.C. Ferry Corporation, has the potential for creating drastic change. If there is any hope of preserving the true character of the islands, we must insure that no new species are allowed to enter the archipelago.

Today, introduced raccoons, squirrels, elk, deer, rats, house mice and beaver are spreading towards the farthest corners of the Charlottes, and their

often be seen bounding across a road or foraging along beaches. Compared with marten on the nearby mainland they are light coloured, generally orange. Moreover they are one of the largest and perhaps the most distinctive kinds of marten in North America. Marten probably existed on the Charlottes during the last glaciation. Their large size would have been a particularly useful adaption during those icy times since the smaller surface area to weight ratio would have helped them conserve heat.

The black bear *(Euarctos americana carlottae)* is the largest black bear in North America. It also differs

The majority of extinctions caused by man have been on islands, often through the introduction of new species. On the Queen Charlottes, without natural predators deer browse heavily, beaver alter fragile habitat conditions and tree frogs multiply with untold impact upon insect populations.

effects on the native flora and fauna are certainly being felt. The beaver, by building dams in the flat country of Naikoon Park, are joining lakes that have remained separated probably since glaciation. The different kinds of stickleback fish that have developed in these individual lakes and that offer such a valuable natural laboratory for the study of evolution are being irreversibly altered by such drastic changes to their environment. Deer have dramatically altered the vegetation, and raccoons will cause great havoc should they ever reach the seabird colonies.

The introduction of mink on the Charlottes would also devastate most seabird colonies. Wild domestic goats could cause wholesale destruction of the vegetation as they have done already on the Galapagos and on some of B.C.'s Gulf Islands. Recent squatters on one of the islands in South Moresby left behind a population of domestic goats that may cause serious problems on the Queen Charlottes if they escape to nearby islands.

History should have taught people the dangers of introducing new species to islands. Much of the native life in Australia, New Zealand, the Galapagos and Hawaii has been wiped out by introduced species. And yet it is still happening. The tree frog, introduced near Tlell a few years ago, is still spreading. What its ultimate effect on the Charlottes will be is unknown.

What most distinguishes the Queen Charlottes from continental regions, the essential underlying cause of its biological peculiarities, is the nature of the ecological web that holds all of its diverse elements in place. But we really have no idea how the whole system is put together or how it works. To come up with that secret formula, we would first need to learn a great deal more about the interactions between organisms and their physical environment, and the interactions within and between species. Only then could we begin to have even a chance of understanding.

Meanwhile, the industrial acts of logging, mining and commercial fishing create major gaps in the historical linkages between species, making it virtually impossible to construct an accurate model of the original community of life. We need to conserve the marine and terrestrial habitats of the South Moresby archipelago as an intact coastal ecosystem, not only for the preservation of its genetically diverse kinds of life but also for the potential of yielding insight into evolutionary and ecological processes yet to be conceived.

THE GREEN MANTLE

The plant life of South Moresby is a complex and ancient tapestry. Between the snowy peaks of the San Cristoval mountains and the grassy meadows of tidal river estuaries stretch the colours and textures of more than one thousand kinds of plants. These combine with one another (and with the birds, mammals, insects and fish) in a seemingly endless array of ecological threads.

The awesome thing about this tapestry is that the closer we look, the more interlacing strands we find. And the more we find, the more we realize how little we really know about how the ecosystem works and about the effects of our demands upon it.

Communities of plant species form patterns of association which seem to repeat under similar conditions of climate and geography. In South Moresby, botanists recognize about a dozen different plant assemblages.

At sea level, a narrow fringe of hardy, salt-tolerant vegetation links the marine intertidal community to the coastal forest. Close by is the rain forest, known throughout the world for its huge primeval conifers and soft moss-carpeted understory. These include the climax hemlock forest, the Sitka spruce forest and stands of giant red cedar. In the lowlands, the green glow of conifer swamps reveals luxuriant congregations of mosses, liverworts and fungi. Next are the coastal muskeg wetlands, highly acidic bogs filled with sphagnum moss and a whole new assemblage of plants. On the slopes rising above the bogs are the subalpine parklands of mountain hemlock and yellow cedar. These are followed at still higher elevations by alpine meadows, flowering heaths and rocky steeplands which cap the San Cristoval mountain range, the backbone of South Moresby.

An ancient tapestry of spruce, cedar and hemlock covers the Windy Bay watershed.

49

Tidal marshes are the most productive of the maritime plant communities. Stream estuaries and intertidal mud flats are important foraging habitat for mice, small birds, deer, bears, and a host of migratory and resident waterfowl.

While this general range of plant associations is not unique to the coast, although a fair number of individual plant species are, what is striking about South Moresby is a sense of all of these communities being tightly compressed into a narrow, one-hundred-kilometre-long wedge, the outcome of over ten thousand years of habitat selection and adaptation. It is because of the existence of glacial refugia on the Charlottes that, for longer than on most of the north Pacific coast, all of these species have been trying their hand in a variety of circumstances, sometimes succeeding, sometimes not.

As a result, the plant life of South Moresby forms a compact microcosm of the northwest Pacific coast. A visitor can step ashore in a quiet intertidal estuary, enter the west coast rain forest, traverse the whole range of natural communities up into the alpine, to a vista of the rugged west coast and the open Pacific Ocean, all in a matter of hours.

We have an urgent need to understand this labyrinthine and mysterious tapestry. We must understand it because our economy depends heavily upon it. The urgency is because every day another species or two disappears from our planet. We are quickly removing our old-growth forests in British Columbia, just as we are doing in the tropics and the other ancient forests of the world. Every day we come one step closer to eliminating our natural heritage without ever really understanding what it means.

WHERE LAND AND SEA MEET. At the interface of land and sea is a fringe of maritime vegetation which has adapted to a range of exposure to salt water, wind and surf. The shingle beach is the most common type of shoreline on eastern Moresby

Island. In exposed locations, this substrate of tide-washed gravels and cobblestones supports sparse colonies of hardy sea rocket. Farther up the beach, out of the reach of wave splashing, live more intricate communities of lime grass, beach pea, giant vetch, hemlock-parsley, beach lovage, madder, coast clover and ocean strawberry. More protected beaches show even greater diversity, and the zonation of plant communities — where several species are assembled together in distinct combinations — is conspicuous. These zones are aligned in bands parallel to the water's edge, and typically range from the tidal communities of eelgrass and fucus, through the spring-tide plantain zone, to the terrestrial habitats of hairgrass and sedges, and then the lush grass meadows.

The most diverse and productive of the maritime plant communities are tidal marshes, especially those in stream estuaries or intertidal mud flats such as at Burnaby Narrows. The soils, usually finely textured and nutrient-laden deposits of silt, have enabled a different range of species to take root, such as tufted hairgrass, sea arrowgrass, Nootka reed grass, Baltic rush, Lyngbyei's sedge, sea barley, red fescue and silverleaf cinquefoil. Since most of the coastline of South Moresby is constantly subject to high levels of wave energy, these more sheltered and highly productive marshes are relatively rare. This accentuates the forage value of their many edible plants, making them important habitat for small birds, mice, deer, bears and a host of resident and migratory waterfowl.

Plant communities along the exposed Pacific coast have had to adapt to extremely dynamic conditions on rocky headlands, volcanic sea stacks and cliff faces. The Queen Charlotte Islands have the

highest average wind speeds in Canada, and storms with winds from 80 to 160 kilometres per hour are not uncommon. The hardy plants of the coastal rock habitat withstand the relentless buffeting by wedging tenacious roots into crevices and by adopting a low, spreading growth form that hugs the rock surface. Although they are regularly bathed in ocean spray, the salt water is unusable and plants in this habitat must collect and store precious fresh water from rain and seepage. Thick, waxy leaves or densely haired leaves are adaptations to prevent desiccation. Roseroot, sea plantain, king's crown, hairy cinquefoil, scurvy grass, rusty saxifrage, ocean strawberry, chocolate lily, Alaska harebell, Nootka lupine and salal are typical of the hardy vegetation that thrives in the exposed maritime habitat.

COASTAL STRIP FORESTS. The South Moresby area encompasses 138 islands of all shapes and sizes. For the most part they are clustered in the bays and inlets of a dozen larger islands, or arrayed offshore in miniature archipelagos, providing ample habitat for a distinctive forest community. Since Sitka spruce is the most salt tolerant of the South Moresby conifers, it predominates in the coastal strip forest. On the exposed outer islets such as Anthony Island, Rankine Islands and Tar Islands, Sitka spruce is the only conifer.

The ground cover varies according to local soil conditions but usually includes a substantial layer of mosses, interspersed with clumps of grasses such as Nootka reed grass, swordferns, flowers such as false lily of the valley and calypso orchids, and red huckleberry and salal bushes.

However, the most outstanding feature of South Moresby's coastal strip forest is not its distinctive plant community, but the animal life that it supports, which includes one-quarter of British Columbia's nesting seabirds. About fifty nesting colonies have been found in South Moresby, accounting for about 50 percent of the province's tufted puffins, 50 percent of the Cassin's auklets, 75 percent of the ancient murrelets, and 35 percent of the Leach's storm petrels. There are also colonies of rhinoceros auklets, pigeon guillemots and fork-tailed storm petrels. There are large ancient murrelet colonies on the east coast of Lyell Island and also on Ramsey Island, consisting of some sixty thousand pairs.

Many of these seabirds come ashore and burrow through the moss and soil beneath tree roots, grassy hummocks and rocks to a depth of up to one metre. The ground in such colonies is sometimes honeycombed with nests which can be damaged simply by walking over them. Such fragile habitat is destroyed by harvesting and hauling away trees. For this reason several of South Moresby's seabird nesting colonies are protected as Ecological Reserves; but where industrial timber values coincide with conservation needs, such as at Dodge Point, colonies remain unprotected.

With such concentrations of small birds, it is not surprising that the coastal fringe forest is important habitat for raptors. Peale's peregrine falcons perch in the treetops and sea cliffs above seabird nesting colonies, waiting for prey to feed their own fledgling young. The same holds true for Canada's largest concentration of bald eagles who feed on South Moresby's smorgasbord of seabirds and marine life.

Eagles also use these trees to build their nesting platforms, usually selecting the largest tree in the neighbourhood. A typical nest tree is four hundred

Like many of the plants that grow along the stormy coast of the Charlottes, Sedum *(above) withstands high winds and salt spray by wedging tenacious roots into rock crevices, adopting a low, spreading growth form and having thick waxy leaves to prevent desiccation.*

The striking red lichen Xanthoria *(opposite) favours exposed west coast locations.*

53

South Moresby's 138 islands provide ample habitat for a distinctive forest community. Sitka spruce, the most salt tolerant of the Queen Charlotte's conifers, predominates in the coastal strip forest.

to six hundred years old, sixty metres tall and three or four metres in diameter. It has to be this size to support the massive nests which may weigh as much as one thousand kilograms. Such tremendous weight is the result of many decades of new branches being added, as well as colonization by grasses and other small plants that take root in the excrement of generations of eagles.

Needless to say, such trees rarely survive clearcut logging. Harvesting trees every seventy-five years effectively eliminates eagle nesting habitat for as long as the practice continues, in addition to the several hundred years required to grow replacement nesting trees. Studies conducted in Alaska, in a number of locations with various logging histories, found that "the density of eagle nests corresponds very neatly and inversely to the amount of logging and human disturbance."

A 1978 eagle nest survey in South Moresby found 1.33 nests per kilometre of coastline, the highest density of nests recorded in Canada and second only to Alaska's Admiralty Island (1.4 nests per kilometre). While the U.S. Forest Service requires a one-hundred-metre buffer zone around nest and perch trees from which all industrial activities are excluded, and also requires that future nesting needs are provided for by stipulating that logging plans leave the dominant trees in any stand of likely potential, the same kind of protection is as yet lacking in B.C.

T HE FOREST PRIMEVAL. Stepping up off the beach and into the moss-carpeted forest, you pass into another world. The silence is profound. The pungent odours of salt and kelp give way to

The coastal forest provides nesting sites for large numbers of seabirds and raptors, especially bald eagles. Clearcut logging right to the shoreline— practised extensively on the Charlottes— destroys this critical habitat for many generations to come.

The virgin temperate rain forest, fast becoming one of the rarest ecosystems on earth, is also the least understood. Referred to by industrial foresters as a "cellulose cemetery," it is actually host to such a horde of moulds, algae, fungi, bacteria, insects, mammals and birds—like this varied thrush—that it can be called anything but "dead."

subtler, more fragrant aromas of cedar, spruce and mosses. It is darker here, and the air is noticeably damp. High overhead in the upper canopy the sea breeze still combs the tree tops, but below is an awesome stillness. Shafts of sunlight stream down through moss-festooned branches, dappling the forest floor and playing across the massive trunks of regal Sitka spruce, cedar and hemlock.

This is an ancient forest. Its roots have been tilling rich mineral subsoils for millenia. Mosses and lichens have colonized almost every available surface. Over time they succumb to wind and gravity's pull and fall to the forest floor, there to be digested by insects, fungi and bacteria, and incorporated ultimately into deep loamy topsoils.

The same greeting awaits anything that falls to the forest floor and keeps relatively still. It is embraced by the system, converted, recycled endlessly. Trees that die still standing host such an unnamed horde of moulds, algae, fungi, bacteria, insects, birds and the occasional mammal that they can be called anything *but* dead.

The result of this prolonged intermingling of life forms is a consummate ecosystem about which we know very little, and about which some of us pretend to know enough to justify its elimination. This much we do know: these forests are the largest accumulations of biomass (living matter) on the planet, even more so than the tropical rain forests.

L OWLAND FORESTS. The truly phenomenal lowland forests occur on floodplains, where rich soils sustain a riot of mosses, ferns, lichens, moulds, succulents, and every imaginable size, shape and age of tree. Standing dead trees, snags and rotted stumps are common, as are large logs lying on the ground or straddling streambeds. Besides the spruce, colossal specimens of western hemlock and western red cedar grow here, the giants of their genera, among the largest remaining on the coast.

These large old trees play complex ecological roles, providing habitat for many plant and animal communities. They are major movers in the carbon, nutrient and water cycling processes of the forest. Old-growth trees are primary sites for photosynthesis, the transformation of the sun's energy into the biomass upon which the rest of the forest ecosystem depends. A single old monarch spruce may have over fifty million needles, providing a cumulative photosynthetic surface area of over twenty-five thousand square metres. Younger trees perform the same function but on a much-reduced scale.

Having produced and stored such large quantities of biomass over the centuries, mature trees eventually die and yield up their treasures to the ecosystem. Standing snags provide food and nesting habitat for flora and fauna. Fallen logs are blanketed in mosses and infiltrated by cellulose-digesting fungi and nitrogen-fixing bacteria, soon to become "nurse logs" to rows of diminutive spruce and hemlock seedlings. They also support tremendous numbers of invertebrates and are used by small mammals and birds for nesting, feeding and protection.

Fallen logs also have a crucial role to play in freshwater ecosystems. Stretching from bank to bank and partially submerged, such logs stabilize stream banks and beds, and regulate water flow rates, thus maintaining optimum conditions for spawning salmonids and their incubating eggs. They also

provide habitat for aquatic and terrestrial insects, both of which in turn are important food species for foraging young salmonids.

The canopy of a single stand of old-growth trees may be inhabited by over one thousand different species of insects and spiders. Most are the adult phase of species that spend their immature stages on the forest floor, usually inside various plants, decaying wood or aquatic ecosystems. Adult fungus gnats for example, found in great numbers in the upper canopy, live as larvae in the abundant mushrooms on the forest floor.

Most of the surface of an ancient conifer is colonized by epiphytic plants, by numerous species of mosses, lichens and algae. One epiphyte ("growing upon another plant") of tremendous ecological importance is a large, leafy lichen, *Lobaria oregana,* that fixes nitrogen from the air. This nitrogen is ultimately claimed by the entire forest through leaching, litterfall and decomposition. Recent estimates of this function indicate a contribution of from three to five kilograms per hectare, representing about half of the total nitrogen "budget" of a mature forest. It is a striking revelation that this insignificant-looking little plant plays such a keystone role in the largest accumulation of living matter on the planet. Nitrogen-fixing epiphytes are uncommon in a second-growth forest, a factor with undetermined implications for the silvicultural management techniques of British Columbia's "tree farms."

Another source of nitrogen fixation is a bacteria that lives in a symbiotic relationship within the root nodules of red alder. One of the first species to colonize soils disturbed by logging or landslides, red alder has been found to be among the most prolific

nitrogen-fixers in the plant world. The particular form of alder-fixed nitrogen is valuable to conifers, as its presence in soil inhibits the growth of the *Poria weirii* fungus, the principal cause of root rot. But alder is not a commercial species and is also an aggressive grower — invading and dominating some sites disturbed by logging for thirty years or so, after which time the conifers eventually gain succession. Because this thirty-year delay interferes with the growth and yield tables upon which foresters base allowable annual cut (AAC) calculations, it is often viewed by silviculturalists as a weed tree to be disposed of with applications of herbicides such as 2-4-D.

Many foresters are in the habit of considering old-growth forests as "silvicultural slums," "biological deserts " and "cellulose cemeteries." These epithets are hard to understand, given the much greater abundance and diversity of species relative to a second-growth forest. The structural variation, complex vertical stratification and horizontal patchiness of a mature forest like Windy Bay provide a vast range of habitat. By comparison, a young, densely spaced, uniformly aged second-growth forest, planted in soils that in some places have been scarified and burnt, is truly biologically deprived.

Windy Bay, on the northeast corner of Lyell Island, is the archetypal forest primeval, containing a mixture of several plant communities. Its lowland forests have developed upon river terraces and floodplains, nurtured by mineral-rich soils recruited from the upper slopes of the surrounding watershed. The river itself is small yet prolific. Its lower reaches include some eight kilometres of prime salmonid spawning habitat, fed by an intricate maze of smaller tributaries, that are important rearing

Opposite, clockwise from upper left: epiphitic moss, Amanita muscaria, *angelwing fungus, coral-root orchid, red-fruiting* Cladonia *lichen and dwarf dogwood. The astonishing genetic diversity of plant species in a mature ecosystem is lost when reduced to an even-aged stand of commercially desirable trees.*

Both above and below ground, an intricate maze of small tributaries provides stability to water run-off rates as well as pristine water for salmonid spawning and rearing habitat. Opposite: old life sustains new life as each fallen tree becomes a "nurse log" to the next generation of hemlock.

60

habitat for juvenile coho salmon, cutthroat trout, Dolly Varden char and stickleback. Then there are the meadow forests, with few shrubs and a lush, grass-dominated ground cover. The trees are tall and widely spaced and are exclusively Sitka spruce. Combined with the adjacent ancient murrelet nesting colony at Dodge Point, Windy Bay is such an outstanding example of old-growth forest and aquatic communities that it has been proposed as an Ecological Reserve. This would assure future opportunities for aquatic and terrestrial research, retain ancient forest specimens for their genetic and educational values, protect one of the largest nesting sites of ancient murrelets in British Columbia and preserve archaeological and Haida heritage sites.

HEMLOCK FORESTS. Western hemlock dominates the majority of low- and middle-elevation forests in South Moresby. Red cedar is a frequent associate, becoming increasingly dominant under moister and richer soil conditions. Sitka spruce is less constant but occurs widely, often as very old, large trees emergent from the rest of the forest canopy. Yellow cedar becomes an important component of hemlock forests only at middle or montane elevations.

"Climax forest" is the name given to a system that appears to have completed a long process of succession by various types of trees. In South Moresby, one of the key environmental determinants in this process is the amount of shade in which understory seedlings must grow. Western hemlock and red cedar are the most shade-tolerant and eventually come to dominate the overstory. Sitka spruce appears to depend largely on windthrow, landslides,

Sitka spruce six metres in diameter were once common on the Charlottes. Most of these old monarchs are gone now, except for a few remnants in isolated places like Windy Bay. Even the few which are left, the giants of their genera, are slated for harvest in the near future.

insect infestation or fire to create openings in the canopy.

The hemlock forest normally forms a dense sunscreen, although climax stands typically have uneven canopies with occasional gaps that allow localized penetration of light. Dark green mosses and liverworts carpet the forest floor, and epiphytic mosses and lichens are abundant. There is a conspicuous lack of understory shrubs and herbs, a function of the prevailing deep shade and of browsing by deer. Typical shrubs are blueberries, red huckleberry and false azalea. Characteristic herbs include deer fern, spiny wood fern, twayblade orchids, twisted-stalks, fern-leaved gold thread and single delight.

Sitka spruce forests. Although hemlock is the most abundant tree on the Charlottes, people invariably associate massive Sitka spruce with the "Misty Isles." The Haida used spruce extensively, splitting its long, tough root fibres and weaving them into water-tight hats, baskets, fishing nets and lines.

The spruce forests of the Charlottes have several features that distinguish them from their counterparts on the mainland. Their distribution is more extensive than in other coastal areas, because of their salt tolerance and the great length of shoreline on the Charlottes exposed to offshore winds from all directions. They also have produced the finest quality spruce wood in British Columbia.

This characteristic did not escape the notice of the early timber industry. The superior strength-to-weight ratio of spruce made it highly desirable for airplane structural members, and thus many of the finest and largest spruce were conscripted into the Allied air forces during the First World War. Most of the big trees harvested in this era were removed by "A-frame," dragged off the slopes and boomed up in adjacent estuaries and bays. It is only because the Windy Bay estuary faces the prevailing southeasterly storm winds, making it impossible to prepare logs for transport, that its large spruce were spared the axe.

Today, spruce logs of exceptionally high-quality are purchased whole by instrument makers for guitar and violin tops. A single, twelve-metre-long, clear-grained log with eight growth rings per centimetre, now only a memory in the forests of Japan and Europe, is worth as much as seventy-five thousand dollars.

Most of the old giants are gone now. All but the most scattered pockets of spruce, nestled in isolated watersheds, have either been cut or are charted for eventual removal. On industrial forest land, where trees are cropped on relatively short rotations, the massive spruce will probably never have the opportunity to grow back again. Those that remain are an increasingly rare and invaluable part of our natural heritage.

Red cedar forests. Western red cedar is predominant in low elevation forests that are either wetter or drier than normal. They are most often found on well-drained ridge tops and steep upper slopes, especially on the small islands on the east coast of South Moresby. Shore pine, a coastal variety of lodgepole pine, also has this ability to adapt to moisture extremes, and is a frequent resident in less productive red cedar forests. The west-

ern yew, a very dense wood with a beautiful carmine-orange patina, also grows in this community, preferring sites along moist yet well-drained slopes. Its broad, flat needles lend it the shade tolerance required for its position as a smaller understory tree.

Scrubby, mixed forests of cedar and hemlock have colonized poorly drained, flat and undulating terrain on the east coast, as well as the steeper land on the exposed west coast. These are forests of relatively low productivity, the result of wet, acidic soil conditions. Salal, deer fern and bunchberry are typical understory plants. Frequent pockets of sphagnum indicate that these forests may be in a state of transition to wetland bogs.

While there is concern over conservation of spruce on the Charlottes, there is consternation over the future of western red cedar. When deer were introduced at the turn of the century, little thought was given to the potential effects of letting loose an exotic species in an ecosystem devoid of natural predators. On many logged-over sites, where deer are fond of browsing on young trees and shrubs, the rate of cedar regeneration is less than one percent of its former natural level. Most timber companies have abandoned attempts to replant with cedar, both because of deer and because there is little commercial value in the small size of cedar trees produced in eighty years, which constitutes the present rotation period on the Charlottes.

There are also disturbing cultural ramifications to this problem because the cedar is the cornerpost of Haida culture. As Bill Reid says in his book, *Out of the Silence:*

If mankind in his infancy had prayed for the perfect substance for all material and aesthetic needs, an indulgent god could have provided nothing better. Beautiful in itself, with a magnificent flared base tapering suddenly to a tall, straight trunk, wrapped in reddish brown bark like a great coat of gentle fur, gracefully sweeping boughs, soft feathery fronds of grey-green needles.

Huge, some of these cedars, five hundred years of slow growth, towering from their massive bases.

The wood is soft, but of a wonderful firmness and, in a good tree, so straight-grained that it will split true and clean into forty foot planks, four inches thick and three feet wide, with scarcely a knot.

Across the grain it cuts clean and precise. It is light in weight and beautiful in colour, reddish brown when new, silvery grey when old. It is permeated with natural oils that make it one of the longest lasting of all woods, even in the damp of the northwest coast climate.

When steamed, it will bend without breaking. It will make houses and boats and boxes and cooking pots. Its bark will make mats, even clothing. With a few bits of sharpened stone and antler, with some beaver teeth and a lot of time, with later a bit of iron, you can build from the cedar tree the exterior trappings of one of the world's great cultures.

Today, Haida culture is enjoying a renaissance of its artforms, manifest in new poles, canoes and long-houses being carved for their own purposes as well as an international market. As old-growth cedar stands are eliminated by harvesting, and as unlogged veterans eventually age and die, they will not be replaced to any great extent by either plantations or natural regeneration. Without some form of control or protective measures the demise of the large western red cedar is inevitable. Special and costly effort is going to be required to ensure a supply of high-quality, old-growth red cedar for this and future generations of carvers, not to mention foresters, biologists and naturalists.

The western red cedar, cornerpost of Haida culture, is a disappearing species. In the past, Haida forest use included boring a test hole to determine a cedar's soundness for canoe construction; unsuitable trees were left growing in the forest. Where the Haida cut little and utilized everything, modern logging cuts everything and wastes much.

Muskeg is a highly acidic environment which provides little in the way of nutrients, yet many plants have adapted to such conditions superbly: (opposite, clockwise from upper left) Andromeda, the insectivorous sundew, cloudberry and sphagnum moss, bog cranberry and sphagnum, yellow water-lily and swamp laurel.

WETLANDS. Coastal bogs are the most abundant wetland community in South Moresby, and occur on flat or gently contoured areas with heavy precipitation and poor drainage. The predominant species in the bog is sphagnum moss, whose gradual accumulation has formed the soft, rolling hummocks so characteristic of this habitat. As successive generations of sphagnum grow over top of one another, a deep layer of partially decomposed "peat" is formed, up to several metres thick. This peat blanket acts like a sponge, holding a great quantity of water and binding scarce nutrients in an anaerobic and extremely acidic medium. Many plants and other life forms have special adaptations to allow them to survive in such an acidic environment, such as the tiny, insect-eating sundew plant, which absorbs water from its prey.

Bogs occur over a few flat areas of the eastern regions of South Moresby, mostly on Lyell and Burnaby islands. Stunted, shrubby lodgepole pine and red cedar are the most common tree species. It is the gnarled little pine that has earned muskegs the epithet "bonsai bogs," after the Japanese art of carefully cultivating artificially miniature trees (bonsai) over many generations. Growth in the muskeg is naturally limited by the lack of nutrients, resulting in pine trees several hundred years old which are often no larger than one metre high, with trunks only ten or fifteen centimetres in diameter. The wood in such a tree has a very high resin content, and when cut it has the feel of polished petrified wood, its tiny growth rings almost indistinguishable from each other.

Bogs have a fascinating microtopography, with complex textures and colours that confound one's sense of scale. Most visitors sooner or later end up on their hands and knees exploring the Lilliputian domains found on raised hummocks. Pit ponds and more extensive pools contain skunk cabbage, yellow water lilies and various pondweeds, occasionally nibbled back by sandhill cranes or foraging deer. Numerous small rills and streams drain the ponds, snaking between thick lawns of sphagnum moss and islands of stunted forest with such typical shrubs as Labrador tea, bog laurel, salal and juniper.

Blanket bogs develop in humid, maritime climates, where they cover both flatlands and slopes of considerable steepness. They occur over much of southern Moresby Island, and are especially widespread on the west coast. The vegetation is similar to that of the other bog types, except that yellow cedar and mountain hemlock associate at lower elevations, especially on the west coast. Although sphagnum moss is present, dense mats of sedges become an important ground cover. The layer of accumulated peat is quite shallow, and in many places bare rock and mineral soil are exposed.

On the west coast, blanket bogs are frequently continuous from sea level up to the alpine and contain a greater diversity of flora. Mountain daisy, false hellebore, alpine azalea, partridge foot and other subalpine plants are frequently found at low elevations.

SUBALPINE FORESTS AND PARKLANDS. On the east coast of South Moresby, the composition of the forest changes gradually with altitude. At the six-hundred-metre elevation, the transition into subalpine forest is abrupt. Western hemlock and Sitka spruce are rare, and red cedar is replaced by mountain hemlock and yellow cedar, which grow in a charac-

The subalpine zone ranges from lower elevation forests of gnarled lodgepole pine, such as surround Lower Victoria Lake, to higher elevation parklands. Expansive heath meadows containing Dodecatheon *and the broad-leafed false hellebore occur around the eight-hundred-metre level.*

teristic short, tapering shape. This is a fairly open forest, with typical understory shrubs of blueberries, huckleberry, false azalea and copperbush.

Sitka alder, or slide alder, is abundant in gullies and avalanche tracks, where tiny nitrogen-fixing microbes, living in a symbiotic relationship within the root nodules of alder, help build new soils for another generation of plants.

The subalpine forest thins out noticeably at elevations near eight hundred metres, where snow loads are greater and take longer to melt. Scattered stands of conifers open up to expansive heath meadows; here three kinds of white heathers (clubmoss, Steller's and Merten's), yellow mountain heather and dwarf blueberries form a dense, low ground cover. Other plant species with more showy blossoms are Newcombe's butterweed, mountain daisy and beaked lousewort.

THE ALPINE. High in the steep and rugged peaks of the San Cristoval mountains is a stunning alpine vegetation zone. The cool, moisture-laden atmosphere of Pacific fog and storm clouds nurtures a carpet of alpine heaths and meadows studded with rocky outcroppings and cliffs. The alpine zone is usually found above the eight-hundred-metre mark, but alpine-like vegetation often ranges down to the three-hundred-metre elevation on the west coast.

Alpine heath is the predominant plant community, with its thick, springy cover of white and yellow heathers, black crowberry, partridge foot, alpine azalea and dwarf decidous blueberries. Near the treeline, the heath may contain clumps of krummholz — stunted and gnarled mountain hemlock and yellow cedar.

The alpine meadows of South Moresby are a lush, intense green, and are dominated by herbs and grasses. Typical species are Nootka reed grass, sedges, and herbs such as arrow-leaved butterweed, cow parsnip, mountain daisy, false hellebore, shooting star and broad-petalled gentian.

The final alpine community, and perhaps the most interesting in botanical terms, is found among rocky outcroppings, cliffs, boulderfields, steep talus slopes, gullies and snow avalanche tracks. It is these remote and unlikely places that, along with isolated seashore knobs and cliffs, most likely formed the "nunataks" within the Cordilleran ice sheet. Poking up out of the flow of the glaciers, these areas may have been snow-free for several months of the year, long enough to serve as refugia for hardy plants. Although the plant cover is sparse and discontinuous, these rocky areas have a rich flora that contains many of the rare and the endemic plants of the Queen Charlottes. A selection of typical species includes parsley fern, Cooley's buttercup, various saxifrages, caltha-leaved avens, mountain sorrel, twinflower violet and Savile's isopyrum. Here also can be found the endemic saxifrage, alpine lily and Newcombe's butterweed.

From the alpine vegetation of the San Cristoval summits to the salt-hardy fringe of maritime plants, South Moresby is blanketed by a verdant mantle which is still largely undisturbed by the industrial activities of man. Few locations in British Columbia present such a diversity of vegetation zones compressed into so small an area. As such places are being progressively eliminated, it is a timely challenge to our professional foresters and politicians to insure that forest lands are managed not only for industrial tree farming but also for the conservation of exceptional representations of our natural heritage.

We need such reserves, both for the things they might someday teach us and our children, and because such grand old communities have a right to exist simply for their own sake, the sovereign natural communities of our planet earth.

The cloud-wrapped alpine meadows of South Moresby are a lush carpet of herbs, grasses and heathers, and contain many of the rare endemic plants of the Queen Charlottes.

LIFE ON THE ROCKS

One cannot understand the South Moresby Island wilderness area without understanding the sea, for their stories are inextricably linked. As the sea washes in and out among these enchanted islands, each wave, each rising and falling tide inspires among onlookers a sense of renewal. Here, the sea makes an indelible impact on the landscape and its life. Waves and moving water carve relentlessly at solid bedrock, creating a new and austere scene at every turn of the shore. Salt spray from crashing waves blows against hillsides, stunting the growth of trees. Animals come to the shore at low tide, the deer to nibble at seaweeds, the bear to capture crabs from overturned rocks, the eagle to pick off small abalone. Every living animal and plant on the islands is somehow linked to the sea and its life patterns, often more directly than we might imagine.

Within the sea itself, life is a complex maze of interconnected food webs, each animal and plant linked through a series of eat-or-be-eaten relationships. It would be difficult indeed to trace precisely the complicated relationship between, say, a whale and a barnacle. But it would also be unrealistic to view either of these organisms as separate unto itself.

Consider the sei whale, a baleen-feeding animal which is totally dependent upon large crustaceans and small fish of the open sea for its food. These animals in turn feed upon tiny planktonic crustaceans and the myriads of planktonic larvae produced by bottom-dwelling creatures. Barnacles on the shore feed upon these same planktonic forms and, at certain times of the year, spew out countless numbers of their own larvae. Shore barnacles, then, are indirectly either competing against sei whales for

Each wave, each rising and falling tide inspires in the viewer a sense of renewal.

73

Like the towering rain forest on land, Nereocystis (opposite) forms giant kelp forests offshore. Kelp provides food and habitat for an incredible variety of sealife. The shrimp Pandalus platyceros (above) is just one of more than a hundred thousand creatures per square metre that have been found living on kelp fronds.

food or creating sei whale food through their own reproductive activities.

The sea is a place full of many such fascinating interconnecting tales, of constantly changing life-balances. Organisms living on the shore, between the imaginary lines that mark highest and lowest tides, are ideal subjects for the amateur or professional naturalist who wishes to observe and understand interrelationships among living things.

About 1600 kilometres of shoreline in the South Moresby region embody almost every type of shore habitat imaginable: exposed rocky shores and sandy beaches, protected and semi-protected rocky intertidal regions and a spectrum of mud or mixed mud and rock shores. Muddy shores are found in the inner reaches of the region's many deep inlets where streams deposit their fine sediment into a quiet water. These are the estuaries, especially important environments for waterfowl, shorebirds and salmon migrating in and out of streams.

There are over fifty salmon spawning streams in the South Moresby region, providing habitat for pink, chum, coho and one run of sockeye salmon, plus steelhead and cutthroat trout and Dolly Varden char, and a number of other resident freshwater species. After hatching out in April and May, the chum and pink salmon immediately travel downstream to the estuary where they spend their first summer before moving out into deep water. Estuaries are extremely productive environments dominated by a flowering plant called eelgrass. Dense beds of eelgrass provide ideal habitat for the young salmon who in turn provide food for the great blue herons and sandhill cranes frequently seen in the southern Charlottes.

The isolated pocket beaches of South Moresby,

though much smaller than the long stretches of sandy beach found on Graham Island, are extremely interesting. Biologically, the intertidal portion of a sandy beach is desert-like; few species can survive in this constantly shifting and abrasive environment. Higher up, in the upper reaches of the splash zone, the pocket beaches of Woodruff and Howe bays present a dynamic story of ecological succession. Windblown sand and salt continually alter the landscape, creating new dunes and wiping out patches of colonizing plants with every storm season.

Another biologically deserted intertidal realm is the boulder beach where wave action is strong. These shores are like giant stone-tumblers, rounding, polishing and sorting rocks into uniform beds. The beauty in these beaches is more musical than biological. On the South Moresby shores of Louscoone Inlet and Kunghit Island, I have heard a dozen different sounds from as many beaches, ranging from gentle whisperings to a frightening, deafening clatter.

Yet when these same rock types occur along a beach with little wave action, they create an environment of tremendous biological abundance. Such rich boulder shores are scattered throughout the South Moresby wilderness. They are dominated by barnacles and bay mussels, short seaweeds and eight-plated chitons. In the interstitial spaces between and under rocks there is often a build-up of healthy organic mud, home for a host of invertebrates including clams, segmented worms and broad-clawed porcelain crabs.

I know of no mixed-bottom beach along the entire Pacific coast that can compare in sheer biological wealth to one site in the South Moresby wilderness area. Situated between Burnaby Island and South

Moresby Island, Burnaby Narrows is a fifty-metre-wide channel connecting the waters of Skincuttle Inlet and Juan Perez Sound. Tides flow alternately north and south through this shallow channel, bathing its living inhabitants in a rapid flow of nutrient-rich water from both inlets.

The quantity of life supported by this active environment is astounding. Plankton feeders, of course, are thoroughly encouraged by the ever-replenishing supply of plankton. Many varieties of clams in incredible numbers grow rapidly here and, since they are restricted to an existence near the surface by the generally rocky substrate, make Burnaby Narrows a seventh heaven for clam-feeders.

Sometimes the Narrows are literally crawling with red rock crabs, which feed upon clams by chipping away at the shell edge until they can get at the meat inside. Many sea stars also feed on clams or on other plankton feeders such as barnacles. One day at the Narrows I counted six different species of these predatory starfish in an area of not more than four square metres. Not far away were two separate species of starfish, both sun stars that are predators only on other starfish.

One sea star abundant in Burnaby Narrows, the bat ray star, usually occurs only on open coastal shores. It is found in a remarkable array of colours — purples and dark blues, reds and browns, yellows and oranges, and nearly every hue in between. A group of hundreds of these starfish concentrated in a localized region of Burnaby Narrows must certainly be one of nature's most artistic creations.

Sea stars, in general, are commanding organisms of the seashore. Their flashy colours and fine geometrical patterns stand out among the subtle hues of algae-covered rocks. One favourite is the vermilion star, its geometrical pattern of tabulate plates looking very much like a bowl of raspberries. On South Moresby, I have often found this sea star within the intertidal zone.

Here, in fact, is one of the fascinating marine biology stories of the Queen Charlotte Islands. Animals and seaweeds are often much more accessible in the Islands than elsewhere on our Pacific coast. Working their way through a particularly rich South Moresby intertidal area, seashore naturalists will likely find many species that farther to the south can be seen only by divers. One example, the colourful ringed-top snail, dots the floor of many low tidepools with its brilliant yellow, pink and violet shell. Another species is the huge wavy top snail (the Pacific coast's largest snail), which commonly ranges into intertidal areas of the Charlottes and provides a source of food for eagles.

Turn a boulder in the low tide zone and discover an impressive array of animals: encrusting sponges and colonial sea squirts, colonies of "moss animals" and hydrozoans, chitons with their eight bony plates and sea cucumbers. Sea stars, worms, brittle stars, nudibranchs (sea slugs) and octopuses are other occasional intertidal inhabitants. Scurrying or slithering over and through these seascapes are crabs and flat worms, snails and ribbon worms, segmented worms and beach hoppers. These teeming communities of under-rock life in the low intertidal realm are unmatchable for their colour and diversity.

To find a site with this kind of diversity, one need only look for a rocky shoreline having large boulders and some protection from powerful waves smashing in from the open sea. Such sites are scattered here and there behind reefs, in sheltered coves and along the edges of Houston Stewart Channel.

A wide spectrum of colours and a remarkable diversity of species characterize life on the rocks: (opposite, clockwise from upper left) brittle star, juvenile sunflower star, McIntyre star, basket star, bat stars, adult sunflower star, fish-eating starfish. Life under the rocks is no less diverse or colourful. The segmented worm (above) is a member of the teeming community of life in the lower intertidal realm.

Contrasting with the quiet underwater world, the shores of Kunghit Island are often pounded by waves up to 10 metres. Not far offshore, Pacific storm systems sometimes combine with tidal currents to create monster waves of 35 metres or more.

Growing to phenomenal size on the west coast of Moresby Island, the "California" blue mussel (above) thrives in the pounding surf of Canada's highest energy coastline, while in the silent, fluid realm below, countless delicate, transparent forms wander aimlessly like starships lost in space: (opposite, clockwise from upper left) Stauro medusa, winged nudibranch, squid, flounder, wing-foot snail, medusa jelly, opalescent nudibranch.

Because they are pounded continuously by breaking waves, shores that face the open Pacific hold a few specialized marine organisms rather than a great variety. Biologists have calculated the degree of force actually experienced by animals and seaweeds on these shores as equivalent to a land wind of 1500 kilometres per hour. So it is surprising that living things can actually survive in this realm, let alone grow in abundance. Vast beds of "California" mussels and goose neck barnacles thrive in the middle intertidal regions, while barnacles, limpets and small periwinkle snails dominate the upper shores. In the lower intertidal zone, brown seaweeds bend and flex with the surge; one, the sea palm, resembles a palm tree in a hurricane.

Ecologically, exposed outer coasts are actually quite consistent all along the northeast Pacific; communities of life on an exposed coast in northern California are similar to those of the Queen Charlottes or southern Alaska. What is remarkable about the exposed-coast animals of the South Moresby region, which experiences the highest wave energy of any of our coastlines, is their great size. A one-gallon wide-mouth jar stored at the University of Victoria is barely large enough to hold its single specimen of the "California" mussel collected by researchers on the outer coast of South Moresby Island. This specimen was a giant among giants, the largest of thousands found along just one small section of coastline.

The same factors that encourage diversity along South Moresby shores and lead to impressive sizes of exposed-shore inhabitants largely relate to the oceanographic properties of the region. The Queen Charlotte Islands lie at the very edge of the continental shelf; to the west, the ocean floor drops off to abyssal depths of the open Pacific. Behind the islands, to the east, is a shallow channel, Hecate Strait, where river-borne sediments are deposited, where nutrient-rich freshwater runoff from the mainland is mixed thoroughly into ocean water, and where water temperature builds up in the shallow seas.

The ocean around South Moresby is a mixing pot, especially Houston Stewart Channel and Cape St. James, where water rushes back and forth with the changing tides. As these two water masses are churned together, ideal conditions for the growth of plankton are created. Microscopic plants (phytoplankton) grow and reproduce rapidly in the warm waters; these nutrient-rich plants are in turn fed upon by countless microscopic animals and converted quickly in the oxygen-rich environment into their animal tissues. Both plankton sources provide a continuous food supply for the giants of the outer coast — the mussels and other intertidal organisms that do so well in South Moresby.

Immediately upon entering the sea around South Moresby, a scuba diver or snorkeler will be impressed by one outstanding feature: countless delicate, transparent forms drifting aimlessly like starships lost in space throughout this silent fluid realm. These macroplankton animals, with names like medusae, sea gooseberries, scalps and seawings, are also visible indicators of an abundance of microscopic organisms within the plankton. Many of these lovely forms wander in from the open Pacific; a number of species are rarely, if ever, seen by divers in other coastal waters.

On the east side of Kunghit Island, not far from Cape St. James, I made what will certainly remain my most memorable dive. My companions and I entered the water adjacent to a vertical cliff face

which towered sixty metres above us and extended some unknown depth below the waterline.

There are huge Persian rugs that represent years of work by a master artist and his assistants. As we descended, the wall before us was a more beautiful tapestry than any hand-crafted rug imaginable. Every square centimetre was covered with a mosaic of densely packed animals and lacy red seaweeds. Moss animals (bryozoans) were the dominant organism of the wall, more abundant here than anywhere else I had ever seen. These tufted colonies provide deluxe accommodations for hundreds of species and millions of individual crustaceans and are a food source for the beautifully coloured nudibranchs.

It is quite probable that kelp bed communities in the Queen Charlottes were much more extensive before the time of European contact. This may seem strange since kelp has never been harvested here. The explanation lies with a furry sea mammal and some interesting ecological connections. When early European and American travellers arrived in the Queen Charlottes they discovered a trading bonanza — the sea-otter pelt. For a relatively small price in iron, tools, blankets, copper or decorative beads, they could obtain quality sea-otter pelts that would bring exceptional prices in China. Stories of the fortunes to be made brought more and more traders and hunters to the north Pacific coast.

Sea otters *(Enhydra lutris)* were hunted with total abandon and their populations declined dramatically; by 1911, when an international treaty was signed to protect the species, they were nearly extinct. In the Queen Charlotte Islands of 1780, sea otters may have numbered between five and ten thousand; by 1920 they had been exterminated. The last one was reported to have been killed in 1918 at North Island.

When they were around, sea otters maintained an important ecological balance connected with kelp beds. As predators, they fed upon crabs, fish, clams and mussels but, most importantly, on abalone and sea urchins, herbivorous animals that crop seaweeds, especially young kelp plants. By keeping populations of urchins and abalones in check, the sea otter encouraged kelp to grow. With the extermination of otters, sea urchin populations all along B.C.'s outside coast increased rapidly. Kelp beds declined because a high percentage of the young replacement algae were eaten before they could grow to large kelps.

Sea urchins are versatile creatures. They eat practically any bit of living material that washes against their spines. They can even get food energy from organic molecules in the water. So, despite a general decline in the kelp food source, sea urchin populations continued to survive in abundance. Many South Moresby locations have huge colonies of red urchins extending over a hundred metres.

Biologists have suggested reintroducing sea otters to the Charlottes. In fact, a remnant population left in the Alaska Aleutian Islands and Prince William Sound has multiplied so well that it can now stand to be thinned. An initial experimental transplant from Alaska to Bunsby Islands, Kyoquot Sound, Vancouver Island has produced a population that now seems to be growing and may be firmly established. And, as we might expect, studies indicate that in this new habitat, kelp beds are expanding and sea urchin beds seem to be dwindling.

River otters, which are often mistaken for sea otters, are abundant in South Moresby where they

spend much of their time foraging in shallow seas and along the shoreline. The darker coloured river otters have a relatively thin tail. They often travel about on shore and usually swim along the water surface belly-down. Sea otters, on the other hand, are lighter in colour with thicker tails. They are seldom seen on land and are most often seen travelling on their backs at the water's surface.

At present there are no shortages of marine mammals in the South Moresby area. Breeding groups of the harbour seal *(Phoca vitulina richardii)* are found on many small islands throughout the wilderness. A favourite haulout site is out among the Tar and Agglomerate islands off the east coast of Lyell Island.

Hunted to extinction on the Charlottes for the Chinese fur market of the nineteenth century, the sea otter no longer holds urchin populations in check. Grazing heavily on kelp, urchins have slowly cropped the Charlottes' once-extensive kelp forests. Today, biologists propose to restore nature's balance by reintroducing sea otters.

83

When a kayaker slips quietly in among the stark and twisted volcanic landforms, suddenly ahead, on a white sand and shell beach, a group of seals will squirm and bounce lazily back into the sea. Usually they do not rush immediately away but, innately curious, will hang around watching from a safe distance, waiting for a peaceful moment to return to their sunning spots. It is not unusual for a seal to swim under the kayaks and look up to examine the boats and their inhabitants.

Like the sea otter, harbour seals do not migrate great distances but stick to a local area. They feed upon fish, molluscs and crustaceans. In South Moresby, populations have maintained stable high levels as a result of the abundance of food sources and an ideal habitat.

In June, the harbour seal female gives birth to a single pup weighing about ten kilograms and already capable of swimming and diving. Pups are suckled for about six weeks before they are weaned and left to fend for themselves. The female will mate about two weeks later, but development of the embryo does not begin immediately. Instead, through a process called delayed implantation, the embryo is held at an early stage of growth for two months before it is actually implanted in the uterus. This delay, combined with a gestation period of about seven months, allows the female to give birth in early summer when major storms are least likely to occur.

Steller sea lions live their lives in harmony with the surf-swept coasts of South Moresby, choosing remote and exposed islands as haulout sites. Here they sit for many hours each day, leisurely digesting food, sunning or weathering out a storm. These quiet periods alternate with intense hunting

activities which may require travel far from the site. Sleek and fast swimming, sea lions are superbly adapted for capturing a variety of fish, squid, crab, octopus and other invertebrates. Such a rich diet naturally leads to an impressive build-up of fat and muscle; an adult bull may weigh up to 910 kilograms, an adult female up to 360 kilograms.

In May, large bulls travel to special breeding islands where they establish territories and fiercely defend them against other bulls. Juveniles and smaller bulls are driven to choose different haulout sites. When the females arrive at the colony, they take up residence on the available space within the established breeding territories. After giving birth to

South Moresby's 1600 km of shoreline provide ample habitat for large numbers of harbour seals. Born in June when major storms are least likely to occur, seal pups, like the one above, are capable of swimming and diving at birth.

85

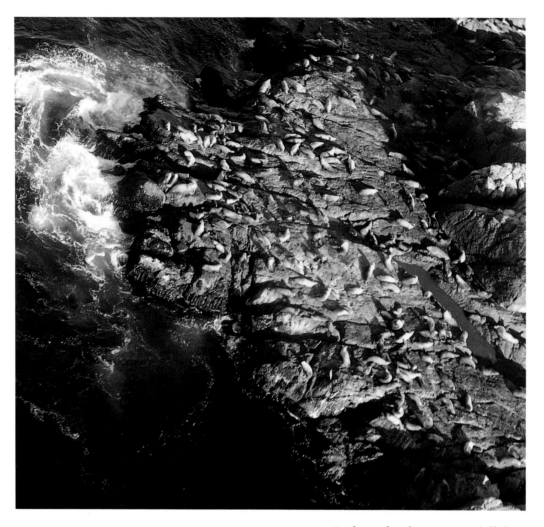

South Moresby is home to over one-half of British Columbia's Steller sea lions. At the remote southern tip of the archipelago, the Cape St. James breeding rookery is the largest on the west coast of North America. Sleek and fast in the water, sea lions can travel far from their haulouts to hunt fish, squid, crab and octopus.

their pup, they later mate with an established bull. Bulls that reign over the best territories usually dominate the largest harems and breed with the larger numbers of females. By the time of pupping, the colony has grown so much that the more desirable territories have the appearance of wall-to-wall sea lions. No wonder, then, that pup mortality rates are extremely high, often 30 percent or more. One false step from a lumbering giant can easily crush a newborn pup.

While this reproductive behaviour has evolved to insure the breeding success of the strongest and fittest members of sea lion populations, it presents some amazing restrictions for the species. For one thing, islands suitable for breeding sites appear to be quite rare. There are only a few sites on Canada's Pacific coast, and only two of any major significance: one on the Triangle/Scott Islands group, the other in the Kerouard Islands immediately to the south of Cape St. James. Here in this most remote corner of the South Moresby wilderness area is the largest sea lion rookery on the Pacific coast. About eight hundred animals haul out each breeding season, giving birth to some three hundred pups.

Whales have great emotional appeal for us, and as our knowledge about them grows, so does our respect. The Haida, the most skilled of all the seafaring Pacific coast people, held whales in high regard. They often hunted the large mammals for food, and it must have been a formidable task to pursue and eventually harpoon a whale from a cedar dugout canoe. Still, much of the whale remains found in middens probably came from animals that had beached themselves or died naturally in the open sea.

But whales have also been hunted in more modern times, and at Rose Harbour on the north end of

Kunghit Island lie the remains of a whaling station which operated from 1910 to 1943. During its operation, thousands of whales were put through the processing plant. It is sad to think of all those great animals towed up Houston Stewart Channel and into the harbour, their bodies hacked into slabs and rendered to oil in the great boilers that still litter the shore.

Houston Stewart Channel has always been a good place to find whales, perhaps the best on the entire Pacific coast. I have observed at least six species in the channel during just a portion of one summer: humpback whales, piked (or minke) whales, orca (or great killer) whales, gray whales, sei whales and fin whales. Both Dall's porpoises and common porpoises were also observed here during the same period.

With two exceptions, great whales are highly transient visitors to British Columbia's coastal regions. They are seldom seen near shores, especially in regions where human developments are present. The exceptions are gray whales, which can now be viewed for most of the year on the west coast of Vancouver Island, and orcas, which tend to travel in localized regions near either end of Vancouver Island.

The study of orca whales on our coast has taken great strides in recent years. We now know that one population type localizes its activities in a relatively small region; their social groupings tend to be large and their habits somewhat predictable. Scientists have learned much about the social interactions and travel behaviour of the area-centred populations.

But little is yet known about the other type of orca populations, those that travel in small pods, usually eight or fewer animals. They do not seem to

concentrate activities in small areas, but move over large ranges that may include most of the B.C. coast. Recent observations indicate that one or two of these transient pods travel frequently to Houston Stewart Channel and Juan Perez Sound. South Moresby will undoubtedly be an important site to study these pods; perhaps such studies will lead to an understanding of how they fit into orca biology on the entire coast.

In a subtle way, whales and dolphins are beginning to be regarded as important monitors of the health of our planet. Since over 70 percent of its surface is covered with water, ours is truly an

Between 1926 and 1943 the Rose Harbour station (above) processed two thousand sperm, blue, fin, sei and humpback whales taken from adjacent waters. It has been estimated that the biomass of the rendered whales was equivalent to the biomass of one million people. Eleven species of cetaceans are found in the area, including three pods of resident Orcinus orca — killer whales (opposite).

89

Above: the white-lined nudibranch, the only species that eats snails; opposite, the decorated warbonnet fish.

"ocean" planet. If all of the contours on its rocky crust were levelled off, the planet would be totally covered with over three thousand metres of water. Slowly, the concept of "Planet Ocean" begins to invade our earth-biased attitude, and we look to knowledge of whale biology, or even simply the experience of seeing these "gentle giants" in their natural habitat, as a new symbol to help us better understand ourselves. Gone is the ferocious great white whale of Melville's *Moby Dick,* symbol of a constant struggle between nature and the human psyche.

INDUSTRY AND THE OCEAN. It is timely to consider the possible impacts of the petroleum industry on South Moresby. About eight hundred thousand barrels of oil a day are shipped southward from Alaska to Washington and California, passing close by the Queen Charlottes, occasionally fouling shorelines with bilge pumpings. And the oil transport industry holds a safety record that is even more fragile than the ecosystems it endangers. The threat of potential losses now looms larger than ever as the governments of British Columbia and Canada give serious consideration to drilling for offshore oil in nearby Hecate Strait, where stormy seas can swell to as high as thirty metres.

One major oil spill can literally destroy what has taken nature at least ten thousand years to build up. The scenario is indeed gruesome: agonizing death for virtually every seabird fouled by oil, for even a small amount of oil clogs up preening glands and disrupts a bird's ability to regulate excretion. It is likely that hundreds of thousands of seabirds would be killed, and major breeding populations would be

A pair of opalescent nudibranchs crawling among solitary orange cup-corals illustrate the intricate beauty and vast array of lifeforms found in South Moresby's still pristine marine environment.

completely wiped out. Sea lions and seals would suffer as well, especially the pups.

As the toxic oil products dissolved in the seawater, much of the plankton and fish would be killed and the loss felt throughout the food chain like a shock wave. Where thick floating oil washed ashore, species in the middle and upper intertidal zones would be destroyed. Sensitive animals such as the herbivore molluscs would be the first to die. Organisms such as crabs might survive but with relatively high concentrations of carcinogenic chemicals stored in their tissues which would be absorbed into the food chain. Eagles and falcons, if they managed to avoid being fouled by oil, would have to seek out new territories. Other shore predators, from oyster catchers to black bears, would face starvation unless they managed to find room on other parts of the islands. Little of the South Moresby we know today would remain.

A more immediate threat to the waters of South Moresby is the damage logging can create. Certainly, steep-slope logging often results in landslides, and landslides destroy sea life by smothering that life under a mountain of debris. The animals and plants on the sea floor fare no better from log booms; as tree bark accumulates on the ocean floor,

species such as the burrowing sea anemone, the sea pen, clams, cockles and sea stars are smothered. More drastic again is the situation where log booms in shallow coves settle on the ocean floor at low tide and crush all living things beneath them. Even a single heavy piece of wave-tossed driftwood can do severe damage to mussel beds and other intertidal communities along the shoreline, and there are many hundreds of thousands of drift logs along the British Columbia coast.

No doubt in future years, as the value of our wild places and their inhabitants becomes more widely appreciated, many people will seek natural places, free from the rumble of engines and the jostle of elbows. South Moresby offers people that opportunity, the opportunity to reflect in tranquillity upon the intricate beauty and biological wonder of a vast array of life forms sharing a tiny piece of the world. But it is a fragile piece of the world and must be handled with great care.

The surrounding ocean is the key to the unique array of ecosystems in South Moresby, and it is also the most vulnerable. It is frightening to think that one serious human error could be enough to permanently upset this precise balance of nature.

WINGS OVER THE WATER

THE SEABIRDS. Of all the animals associated with the world's vast oceans, seabirds are the most visible and familiar. Only about 3 percent of the 8600 known species of birds in the world are seabirds, yet they far outnumber land birds — a not too-surprising fact considering that 71 percent of the earth's surface is covered by water.

True seabirds live exclusively on the ocean except during summer nesting periods, so most of what we have learned about them comes from studies done during their short visits to land for breeding. We know that all seabirds eat animal food, mainly zooplankton, crustaceans and fish. Because they encounter little competition, seabirds have long life spans, low adult mortality rates, late sexual maturity and small egg clutches. They are colonial and monogamous, and most do not defend their nests.

In order to successfully invade the immense, salty ocean environment, seabirds over millions of years have developed physical structures and habits to enable them to fill different niches and roles within the marine ecosystem. The most obvious adaptations include webbed feet, dense feathers, underlying layers of fat (for both insulation and food reserves) and a preening gland for oiling feathers.

For years, however, a great mystery surrounded the question as to how seabirds managed to ingest seawater. It was even rumoured that they flew to large coastal lakes at night for fresh water. Finally, in the 1960s, two small organs were discovered over seabirds' eyes. These "salt glands" are capable of processing the high concentrations of various salts that occur in seawater, and this solution is then simply expelled from the bird's bill.

A lone pigeon guillemot, one among a million South Moresby seabirds.

95

Seabirds rear their young during the warm summer months when days are long and food-rich plankton blooms are spectacular. The glaucous-winged gull chick may live up to thirty years, during which time it consumes large quantities of food and returns nitrate- and phosphate-rich feces to the ocean's nutrient economy.

Ocean hunting grounds are exceedingly productive regions for seabirds. Hectare for hectare, shallow nearshore ocean produces as much living matter as the most fertile land. Still, the seemingly uniform habitat of open ocean does not provide an unlimited or always readily accessible source of food, and some parts of the world's oceans are "avian deserts." The Pacific Ocean is home to the largest concentration of seabirds in the world, nearly half of all species, and it is a very productive body of water; yet even there seabirds have a risky and difficult existence.

The interaction between sea, land and atmosphere is as complex as it is unpredictable. Ocean temperatures vary from year to year, nutrient levels fluctuate, and vagaries of weather alter the amount of sunlight reaching the water surface. Changes in rainfall influence the amount of mineral salts poured into the oceans by major rivers. And changing ocean currents may take food supplies far from searching birds.

All plant and animal life in the surface layers of the sea depends on the presence of dissolved nutrient salts, mainly nitrates and phosphates. These are thrust to the surface by massive upwelling currents, where they are mixed by winds and surface currents and energized by the sun. Microscopic plants called phytoplankton, the foundation of all marine food chains, then absorb them. Areas of turbulence and upwelling yield the richest supplies of surface feed.

Seabirds are affected, one way or another, by the whole range of oceanographic changes. In the Queen Charlottes, their numbers and distribution each year are influenced directly by events in the Gulf of Alaska. Water there circulates in a coun-

terclockwise direction, driven mostly by winds. These same winds and currents, plus occasional storms moving through the gulf, insure thorough mixing of the all-important nutrient salts. The resulting abundant plankton growth provides a rich food source for Queen Charlotte birds as it swings down past the northwest corner of Graham Island on its way back out to sea.

Seabirds also play an important role in contributing to the nutrient economy of oceans. One American biologist has estimated that there are up to forty-five million seabirds off the west coast of North America each summer. They consume 2.5 million tonnes of food and return 1.5 million tonnes of feces to the ocean. This significant contribution of nitrates and phosphates helps to sustain phytoplankton production, which in turn provides the energy that links various food chains in the ocean.

It is no accident that breeding and chick-rearing happen during late spring and the long days of early summer. In these times of warmth and sunlight a spectacular plankton bloom takes place throughout Queen Charlotte waters, supporting large fish stocks. Not only is there more plentiful food for seabird chicks but also the adults need to expend less time and energy fishing and so can take better care of their young. By late summer, however, the nutrients are exhausted, the bloom fades and fish supplies dwindle.

The fifty or so species of seabirds associated with the Queen Charlotte Islands can be divided into three groups: passage migrants, visitors and breeders. Passage migrants visit the Charlottes en masse every spring and fall on their annual migration; they include such long-distance travellers as jaegers, terns, phalaropes and certain gulls. Of the

twelve visiting species, albatrosses and shearwaters breed in the southern hemisphere during the November-to-January "summer" and then move northward in immense flocks to spend the "winter" feeding in cool, food-rich northern waters.

But it is the twelve species of breeders that most people think of when they talk about the seabirds of the Queen Charlotte Islands. These breeding populations fluctuate from perhaps four hundred thousand to as high as one million pairs.

Colonies are established for both geographical and biological reasons. All seabirds on the Charlottes, except the marbled murrelet, breed on the seaward slopes of a myriad of islands. The distribution and size of breeding sites depends on the number, location and size of available islands, the type and quality of vegetation on them and, of course, their proximity to feeding grounds.

In 1977 a field party from the British Columbia Provincial Museum visited every island in the Queen Charlottes to locate seabird colonies and estimate populations. They estimated about half a million pairs of seabirds breeding on nearly one hundred islands. Major breeding stations, those with over twenty-five thousand breeding pairs, include Langara, Frederick, Hippa, Anthony, Lyell and Louise islands, Kerouard Islands and Rankine Islands. Together these account for nearly 60 percent of all breeding seabirds on the Charlottes. The Moresby group, with over 70 percent of all breeding islands, supports about 60 percent of the total breeding population.

Ten species commonly breed on both the Graham and Moresby island groups: two storm petrels, a cormorant, a gull and six alcids. Two others, the common murre and horned puffin, breed only in the Moresby group.

Storm petrels are the world's smallest oceanic birds. They are often called "sea swallows" because of their light, buoyant flight and small size. The two species — fork-tailed and Leach's — account for more than a fifth of the seabirds on the Queen Charlottes; nearly 80 percent of them nest on the many forested islands off the east coast of Moresby. The Leach's storm petrel, the darker of the two, is also the more pelagic, spending much of its time far out to sea. The light grey fork-tailed, on the other hand, is more often seen along the coastline. Storm petrels feed exclusively on various kinds of zooplankton, and both species excavate burrows in the soft soil of spruce forests. In order to reduce their vulnerability to avian predators, they visit the colony only at night.

They both lay a single, white egg, the fork-tails in May and the Leach's perhaps a month later. Both sexes share the extremely long incubation and a fledgling period of four to five months. Interestingly, incubation can safely be interrupted for as much as several weeks if the adults need to be away feeding at sea.

The chicks, covered with thick down, are hatched blind. Within two months they outweigh their parents, who then abandon them. For the next week or two the chicks remain in the burrow, living off their fat, but eventually they scramble down to the shore and begin a two- or three-year odyssey, roaming the oceans of the world while growing to adulthood.

One of the unsolved mysteries of burrow-nesting seabirds that exchange incubation duties at night is how they locate their particular nest entrance among

Above: a rhinocerous auklet and burrows. Freedom from predators and abundant food from the ocean have made South Moresby one of the most prolific seabird nesting areas on the Canadian Pacific. Tiny Rankine Island (opposite) is honeycombed with the burrows of petrels, auklets and murrelets.

The pelagic cormorant has a greater reproductive capacity than any other seabird. The female lays up to six eggs at once and can, if necessary, lay a second clutch to replace stolen or damaged ones.

The striking plumage of the tufted puffin is but a temporary costume. Following the breeding season its bright red beak is lost, its distinctive plumage is molted, and the Charlottes' eight-thousand puffins disperse widely out to sea.

the thousands in the colony. One ornithologist suggests that they use ultrasonics, or perhaps communicating calls between mates. Others argue that they simply locate burrow entrances by keen sight.

Three species of cormorants frequent the Charlottes, but pelagic cormorants — less than five hundred pairs — are the only ones that nest there. The small, widely distributed colonies are located on hard-to-reach ledges of vertical, rocky cliffs. When feeding, these birds make a typical jackknife dive from the ocean's surface and swim with both feet and wings as they chase bottom-dwelling fish. Surprisingly, their feathers are not very waterproof, so they enter the water only to fish and stay only long enough to catch their prey. After they have been diving they can be seen on land with outstretched wings, drying their plumage.

The reproductive potential of pelagic cormorants is greater than that of any other seabirds. They lay clutches of up to six eggs and can, if necessary, lay a second clutch to replace stolen or damaged ones. The North American population centre for this species lies north of the Charlottes on another archipelago, the Aleutians, where some ninety thousand pelagic cormorants are known to breed.

Of the eighteen species of gulls in British Columbia only one, the glaucous-winged, nests on the Charlottes, and a surprisingly small number actually breed there — only two thousand pairs. The largest of the fifty-six colonies is on the Anthony Island group which has 247 breeding pairs.

Glaucous-winged gulls are omnivorous and opportunistic. They feed on a wide variety of items, from offal and garbage to schooling fishes and marine invertebrates. Although they rob eggs from other open-nesting seabirds, especially cormorants, they are not an important seabird predator on the Charlottes because there are so few of them.

There are eight more species of seabirds in the Queen Charlottes, all members of the alcid family. This group of diving seabirds live only in the colder regions of the Northern Hemisphere and together make up nearly three-quarters of the seabirds that breed on the islands. They include both our most-numerous and least-known species.

The range of nesting strategies within the alcid family is remarkable. Common murres lay their single egg on the bare ledges of rocky islands whereas ancient murrelets, Cassin's auklets and rhinoceros auklets excavate burrows in coastal forests. Tufted puffins, on the other hand, prefer to dig their burrows in grassy slopes. Pigeon guillemots and horned puffins simply nestle their eggs into rock crevices. No one knows for sure where marbled murrelets nest in British Columbia, though there is some evidence to suggest that they nest in the lichen-covered branches of coniferous trees.

The Queen Charlotte Islands are the southern limit for its most abundant breeding species, the ancient murrelet. Over two hundred thousand pairs nest in old-growth forests on the larger islands. Like the other forest-dwelling alcids this murrelet is nocturnal.

In late March returning murrelets gather in immense flocks off the islands where their breeding colonies are located and by early April have begun frequent visits to land. Although all the other burrow-nesting species lay a single, pure white egg, by late April each ancient murrelet female has laid two finely speckled, creamy-brown eggs. For the next thirty-five days the adults take turns incubating the eggs using their brood patches — bare areas, en-

dowed with a rich blood supply, located under the wings on either side of the body.

The young hatch already feathered in thick down. Then a remarkable thing happens. Within two days, before ever having been fed, these little balls of grey fluff scramble and tumble down to the sea on huge webbed feet to join their parents. From the moment they hatch, the chicks are able to feed themselves, and they grow to adulthood on the open ocean, feeding on small crustaceans and fishes.

The Cassin's auklet is the most widespread alcid in the North Pacific and the most pelagic; that is, it spends more time on the open ocean than other alcids. It is a plankton feeder and some years may be as abundant on the Charlottes as the ancient murrelets.

British Columbia is the auklet's centre of population; whereas some 130,000 of these birds breed in California and about 600,000 in Alaska, more than 1,000,000 nest on remote, shrub- and tree-covered islands in B.C. The largest colony in the Charlottes is on Frederick Island, where over 100,000 of them dig their burrows among the salal and spruce trees.

Cassin's auklets incubate their single, small egg on brood patches for about thirty-eight days. For the next forty days the adults work together, feeding their chicks regurgitated shrimp-like animals called euphasids and amphipods. Because the most abundant food supplies may be far out to sea, these auklets have developed "gular" or throat pouches for storing food for their young. Most Cassin's auklets nest on the west coast of the Queen Charlottes, as close as possible to their feeding grounds.

Two elongated white plumes on each side of the head and a blunt, horny knob on top of the bill make the rhinoceros auklet hard to miss. Less than four thousand pairs of these nocturnal alcids breed on the Charlottes, most of them on the Anthony Island group. Estimating "rhino" populations, however, is difficult because it is almost impossible to check the contents of their burrows which are often up to six metres long, twisting and snaking around tree roots, and often riddled with side diversions. The young chicks, hiding at the end of the maze, are fed in the burrow chamber until they are nearly full-grown.

Although the rhinoceros auklet's centre of population is southern Alaska, where perhaps two hundred thousand of these large seabirds breed, during the past decade they have been invading islands along the coast of British Columbia, probably because of fluctuations in fish and squid populations.

Easily the most colourful seabirds nesting on the Charlottes are the two species of puffins, tufted and horned, though only about four thousand pairs, often in mixed colonies, breed here, mostly in the Kerouard and Cape St. James groups. It appears that the availability of suitable nesting habitat — rocky for nesting, grassy slopes for burrowing — limits the number of these recent arrivals to the Queen Charlottes. In winter, puffins disperse widely out to sea and are rarely seen.

The only alcid that is restricted to the nearshore is the ubiquitous black-and-white pigeon guillemot. During the day it hauls out on rocky headlands and islets, but in early morning large flocks collect in shallow waters to catch blennies and sculpins. It selects any natural or man-made cranny in which to deposit its two darkly blotched, off-white eggs.

Guillemots are exceptional parents, covering their eggs during the thirty-day incubation period for an average of 95 percent of the time. This species almost always retains its nest and perch site, as well

The ancient murrelet lays two eggs averaging over 40 percent of the adult's body weight. Upon hatching, the precocial chicks are equipped with fully waterproof down and with feet almost as large as their parents'. They emerge from the nest and scramble over the mossy forest and beach to the sea; by dawn, they have swum up to forty kilometres from shore. True seabirds now, they do not return to land for at least two years.

The black oystercatcher creates an artfully arranged nest with bits of shell. Besides cushioning the egg, the white shell probably reflects the sun and thus prevents the developing chick from overheating on sunny days.

as its mate, from one year to the next. At least one thousand pairs of guillemots breed in loose colonies on the Charlottes, and about three-quarters of these are found on the Moresby group.

Only one colony of common murres, about fifty pairs, is located on the Kerouard Islands of the Charlottes. The scarcity of common murres is due probably to a lack of rocky nesting habitat.

The marbled murrelet is the only alcid that has adapted to nesting well inland. Although it is a common bird of nearshore areas throughout the North Pacific, only four nests have ever been found: two were located on tree branches, one in Siberia, the other in California; the other two were discovered in Alaska on the open tundra of treeless islands. In British Columbia, young murrelets, apparently fallen from their nests, have been found in forests at Stanley Park and Point Grey in Vancouver, Port Hardy on Vancouver Island and near Bella Bella on the mainland coast. The closest nest discovery, however, comes from Graham Island.

Walter Feyer reports that in June 1953 he "felled a large mossy hemlock close to the beach about 1/2 mile east of Masset. From the debris an adult marbled murrelet was taken, dazed but alive. . . . Eggshell fragments were found, with blood in them, indicating advanced incubation. The actual nest site could not be determined, however."

Hundreds, maybe thousands, of these small, chocolate-brown seabirds may nest on the Queen Charlotte Islands, but the person who finally finds the first nesting site will have had to check a lot of limbs on a lot of evergreen trees.

SEABIRDS AND MAN. Each summer up to a million seabirds converge on the Queen Charlottes to breed. They arrive fully equipped through evolutionary change to fill practically every available niche offered by the land and sea. But many changes threaten their lives, including both natural threats, which may be catastrophic and are usually short-lived, and human-related ones, which may also be devastating, but more often are long-lasting and sometimes permanent. Among the natural disasters, the most important is loss of food supplies.

Changes in the temperature, nutrient level and direction of surface waters can create a rapid turnover of plankton, leaving only a small standing crop available to seabirds. Mass starvation and reproductive failures usually accompany these periods of low productivity. Fortunately, in the Northern Hemisphere these "shifts" are uncommon.

Certain other changes in the composition of seawater produce a local phenomenon known as "red tide." This, in fact, has nothing to do with tides but refers to rapid blooms of tiny, usually colourless marine algae called dinoflagellates. They are toxic to many life forms including humans, and when they multiply rapidly into large concentrations they are particularly dangerous to seabirds. Just how the toxins are passed through the various food chains in the ocean is unknown.

Storms are another natural hazard that seabirds must contend with. For surface-nesting species like gulls, cormorants and murres, hypothermia caused by heavy summer rainstorms can wipe out an entire year's chicks.

Equally disastrous effects can result at any time of the year from long-lasting storms that inhibit food

gathering. Hundreds, perhaps thousands, of marine birds, mostly alcids, died of starvation on the Queen Charlottes during severe storms in 1982. Some species, like the fork-tailed storm petrel, were forced inland, and many were picked up exhausted as far east as Prince George, 550 kilometres from the coast.

Predators are a natural part of any ecological system. Mammalian predators include both native and introduced species. The native river otter has learned to catch storm petrels at their burrow entrances at night as the birds exchange incubation duties. In one study nearly one hundred percent of the otter scats collected contained the remains of these tiny seabirds.

The introduction of exotic mammals such as mink, rats, raccoons, ferrets, foxes and feral cats and dogs are all obvious threats to nesting birds. But such non-predators as rabbits and sheep are also a concern since they devour ground cover vegetation, which causes soil erosion and thus damages nesting sites for burrowing alcids. Already two exotic mammalian predators, the raccoon and the Alexandrian rat, are widely distributed throughout the Charlottes. Rats not only prey on adult birds but also raid nests for both chicks and eggs. In the long term they may seriously affect population levels of species such as ancient murrelets. Attempts by island residents to import live mink and European ferrets underline the urgency of educating both residents and visitors to the danger of introducing exotic species.

During the last fifty years, human activities have had a great impact on the subarctic regions of the North Pacific. Acid rain, increased siltation and heavy fishing are rapidly creating a new ecological system. But the most immediate man-made threat to seabirds is from pollution resulting from the exploration, production and transportation of petroleum. Both feather fouling and ingestion are well-known and well-publicized effects.

Less known, however, is the fact that most of the estimated 2.5 million tonnes of oil entering the world's oceans each year are lost in the Northern Hemisphere where most seabirds occur. Most North American oil and gas production, moreover, comes from the northwest, the area of greatest seabird concentration. The activity of bacteria and other organic decomposers of petroleum is greatly inhibited by the low temperatures of these northern climes and thus the effects of a spill can persist for many years. Already, roughly 450,000 seabirds die on the west coast of North America each year from petroleum pollution. This is a significant portion of the standing stock of all marine birds in the area, estimated at somewhat less than twenty-five million.

On land, logging poses the greatest threat to seabirds on the Charlottes; even selective logging can cause erosion and soil instability in nesting colonies. Logging the offshore islands would prove catastrophic to the burrow-nesting alcids there. The preservation of these forested islands as nesting sites and buffer areas for expanding or changing populations is critical. Fortunately, six important islands are protected as Provincial Ecological Reserves (Kerouard, Rankine, Lepas Bay, Hippa, Jeffrey and East Copper), although colonies which coincide with industrial timber land, such as the huge ancient murrelet colony at Windy Bay, are not yet protected.

Seabirds and fish are closely interrelated, and

In the cold water of the north Pacific, retention of body heat is critical for seabirds. A spot of oil the size of a dime can kill a bird by ruining the insulative properties of its down. Each year 450,000 birds die from oil pollution on the west coast of North America.

often changes in the abundance of one affects the numbers of the other. Over the last twenty years the tremendous expansion of commercial fishing in the northeastern Pacific Ocean has affected marine birds there in two ways: starvation due to overfishing, and drowning in drift nets.

Several nations carry on industrial fishing in the northern Pacific Ocean, and it is well known amongst fisheries biologists that commercial fishing has contributed to the extinction of some species of fish. Fish-eating seabirds require certain sizes of fish for their diet; the size varies with the species and age of the birds. When these are unavailable the bird simply starves even though its belly may be full. Also, fish of equal size and weight but different species may not provide the same nutritional value as the preferred prey. Moreover, overfishing tends to reduce stocks of larger predator fish, such as salmon, allowing an increase in smaller fishes, many of which are of no use to seabirds.

It is sometimes claimed that fish-eating birds can easily switch to another food if a preferred prey becomes rare because of overfishing, but this is an optimistic assumption. For example, the red-throated loon that nests on the lakes of South Moresby appears to be completely dependent on a specific fish, the sand lance, for feeding its young during their first three days of life. When this prey is rare or absent the young loons die because all of the the alternate fish prey have a body too wide for the young loon to swallow. We simply do not know if the hundreds of thousands of breeding alcids in South Moresby have a similarly highly specialized diet.

Each year Japanese fishermen set over forty-five hundred kilometres of drift nets north and west of the Queen Charlottes, and each year thousands of diving seabirds, particularly alcids and shearwaters, are entangled in them. Although fishermen attempt to avoid concentrations of feeding marine birds, this problem continues. Other human-related threats such as egg collecting, shooting, the use of seabirds as crab bait, the use of puffin bills for rattles, shoreline development and the snaring of seabirds in sportfishing equipment all contribute to the growing list of threats that seabirds must contend with.

There is a very thin line between extinction and survival for our seabirds. We must learn quickly to appreciate and respect what we have. To quote poet John Fowles: "There seemed many great auks 'til the last one was killed."

THE RAPTORS. Birds of prey have aroused admiration and been held in esteem throughout history, yet they have also been persecuted more than any other group of birds. But over the past thirty years our attitudes have changed as research has helped us understand that avian predators are an integral part of life's equation. Although birds of prey are much like other flying birds, ounce for ounce they are much more powerful; an amazing amount of destructive capacity has been packed into their small, light bodies.

Raptors are either falconiformes or strigiformes. Falconiformes, the larger group, are day hunters and include vultures, hawks, eagles and falcons. Strigiformes generally hunt by night and include all of the owls. They are found on every continent except Antarctica and have invaded all habitats except the open ocean. Thirty-four species of birds of prey are

Every year up to a million seabirds—over a quarter of British Columbia's nesting population—converge on the Queen Charlottes to breed. Others, such as the lesser yellowlegs, utilize the Charlottes as a major stopover and feeding area on the Pacific migratory flyway.

known to occur in British Columbia. Of these, nineteen are falconiformes, eleven of which have been recorded on the Queen Charlotte Islands. Four of the fifteen species of strigiformes have been found there as well.

Raptors rely on a wide variety of prey, and even so-called specialist predators such as the peregrine falcon kill nearly 140 different species of birds. Generalized predators such as the bald eagle prey on a variety of animals extending from marine snails to medium-sized mammals. The number of raptors in a given area is determined by the availability of prey, so raptors never totally destroy their prey populations.

Because the abundance of planktonic life off the coast of the Charlottes attracts large numbers of breeding seabirds, raptors fare exceptionally well here, especially species such as the bald eagle and peregrine falcon that exploit marine environments.

But besides serving up an abundant food supply, the Queen Charlottes also provide raptors with a tailor-made habitat: steep cliffs and slopes, estuaries, open sandy beaches, rivers, protected bays, open ocean and numerous forested and bare islands. In addition, the Charlottes' cool, moist climate with relatively warm winters is ideal for raptors adapted to a resident life along the sea coast.

Five races of North American raptors are found almost exclusively on B.C.'s major islands. The only resident and truly endemic form is the northern saw-whet owl *(Aegolius acadicus brooksi)*, found only on the Queen Charlotte Islands. This is a generally darker and more reddish sub-species than mainland populations.

The goshawk *(Accipiter gentilis laingi)* shows affinities with birds of Vancouver Island, where it is also probably resident. Generally, this coastal island race is much darker than nearby continental populations.

Three other species have coastal races that generally extend from southeastern Alaska through British Columbia to northern Washington. These include the sharp-shinned hawk, the red-tailed hawk and the peregrine falcon.

The ten other species of birds of prey on the Queen Charlottes are the rough-legged hawk, northern harrier, osprey, gyrfalcon, merlin, American kestrel, great horned owl, snowy owl, short-eared owl and, of course, the bald eagle.

THE BALD EAGLE. The only eagle in the world whose distribution is restricted to North America, primarily the Pacific Northwest, is the bald eagle *(Haliaeetus leucocephalus)*. There are an estimated thirty-five thousand to forty thousand of these raptors in Alaska, ten to fifteen thousand in British Columbia and two to three thousand in Washington and Oregon combined. Throughout this area eagles are most abundant along the sea coasts.

Bald eagles are a familiar feature on the Queen Charlotte landscape at any time of year. It is not uncommon to see groups of up to twenty individuals perched together in adjacent trees. Since the marine coast provides food of various kinds year round, the eagles are only partially migratory, and those that do migrate are probably mostly the immatures. Some seasonal movements are probably co-ordinated with fish runs on mainland rivers such as the Skeena.

These 4.5- to 6.5-kilogram birds are best known

Ounce for ounce, the bald eagle is one of the most powerful birds on earth, possessing an amazing destructive capacity in its beak and talons.

as scavengers and carrion-feeders, readily utilizing a dead deer on the road or a whale tossed up on a beach. They pirate fish and birds from red-tailed hawks, ospreys and even peregrine falcons. Yet, as fishermen and hunters, bald eagles are unparalleled. They can catch birds by direct pursuit or snatch them from the ocean or ground.

Bald eagles have been observed walking through salal-choked spruce forests in search of disoriented seabirds such as ancient murrelets. And, unlike eagles elsewhere, Queen Charlotte eagles have learned quite effectively to exploit the food-rich intertidal areas. They are frequently seen moving kelp about in search of crabs, small fish and abalone. In fact, the Queen Charlottes are the only region where bald eagles are known to feed extensively on abalone. One nest examined in South Moresby contained the remains of 357 of these large snails.

Birds make up more than two-thirds of the diet of bald eagles on the Charlottes, most of which are true seabirds. But during the winter months, water-birds, especially scoters, scaup and grebes are important prey. Without a doubt, the bald eagle is the most versatile raptor on the continent.

The eagle population on the Charlottes is roughly estimated to be in the low hundreds. They establish their territories early in the year, sometimes two or three months before the April egg-laying period. During this time their courtship flights are a spectacular sight as they lock talons in mid-air and plummet downward for up to one hundred metres in a series of somersaults.

Eagle nests are most often located in the tops of tall spruce trees within two hundred metres of the shore, and are constructed from sticks and lined with seaweed and fresh coniferous boughs. The largest nest found to date measures three metres across and more than one and a half metres thick. Most nest sites have an open view and clear flight path to the beach.

The nesting season generally lasts from early April to September. The usual clutch size is two eggs, but many nests on the Charlottes hold three eggs, probably the result of an exceptionally abundant food supply. The incubation period lasts about forty days, and nest-sitting responsibilities are shared by both parents. When the young are about ten weeks old they begin to think about flying, and within a week or so they are gone forever from the security of the nest.

Eagle populations in the Charlottes are still healthy and stable. At almost any time the sky can suddenly spring alive with the sound of an eagle churning the air with its broad wings.

T HE PEREGRINE FALCON. Author G. H. Thayer said it best when he characterized the peregrine falcon as "perhaps the most highly specialized and superlatively well-developed flying organism on our planet today, combining in a marvellous degree the highest powers of speed and aerial adroitness with massive strength."

Because of an almost perfect environment and an abundant food supply, the Queen Charlottes support the highest breeding densities for falcons anywhere in the world. In fact, seabirds are so plentiful in the islands that competition for food among peregrines appears to be entirely absent.

These majestic raptors currently enjoy relative freedom from persistent persecution by man and total freedom from mammalian predators. They

There are more eagle nests per kilometre of shoreline in South Moresby than anywhere else in Canada—a reflection of the area's rich food resources. Eagle nesting platforms can be utilized for a century or more and can weigh well over one thousand kilograms. The Queen Charlottes are the only place where eagles are known to fledge up to three young at once and also to feed extensively on abalone; one nest examined contained the remains of 357 abalone.

thrive in the cool, moist climate of the misty isles, and they have access to any number of good nesting sites including cliff ledges and trees. Although most peregrine falcon aeries are distributed irregularly around the islands, some may be as little as half a kilometre apart. The peregrines also enjoy a lot of open space over which to hunt.

Nevertheless, their population varies from year to year. In 1980 the total breeding population was estimated at 152 individuals; Moresby Island accounted for 92 of these. If we add to this total the population of non-breeders which, according to one estimate, approaches 50 percent of the breeding population, the total number of peregrine falcons in the Queen

Swooping down on seabirds in a breathtaking powerdive of 320 km/h, the Peale's peregrine falcon (above) stuns its prey and carries it back to the aerie in talons noted for exceptional size and strength. The discarded wings of an ancient murrelet (below) are the distinctive sign of a peregrine kill. Opposite: although a falcon clutch contains three to five chicks, only one will survive the first winter.

Charlottes in 1980 was about 230 birds, not including nestlings.

Every active falcon aerie is located in the immediate vicinity of a seabird colony. When seabird numbers decline or move to new nesting areas, so do the falcons. The peregrine's nesting activities can last up to half a year. By April, an aerie is established near the top of a high, vertical cliff, often under the roots of a spruce tree growing over the cliff's edge. Sometimes a pair of falcons will adopt nests that have been abandoned by bald eagles or red-tailed hawks.

Most clutches are started in mid-May, and towards the end of June the eggs begin hatching. The young, who are adept at flying by the time they are seven weeks old, are still dependent on their parents for another six weeks or so. Peregrines can begin laying eggs at the age of two years and can continue until they are eighteen.

The peregrine falcon is a predator specialized for one type of hunting — direct pursuit over open country. It takes small and medium-sized birds in full flight, utilizing surprise and the advantage of height and positioning, to follow through on its attack. The falcon's speed while diving at its prey reaches a breathtaking 320 kilometres per hour.

Four kinds of seabirds form the falcon's principal summer diet. Ancient murrelets are plucked from the sky as they leave their colonies in the early morning and fork-tailed storm petrels are targeted when they return from the ocean at dusk; Leach's storm petrels and Cassin's auklets generally meet their end over the open ocean. Shorebirds are an important component of the falcon diet during their migration periods, and waterbirds, mostly ducks, highlight the peregrine's winter menu.

RAPTORS AND MAN. Today, birds of prey in British Columbia are protected by the provincial wildlife act, but laws alone cannot assure the future diversity and stability of the raptor community. Although we can control and act upon some of the direct threats, such as shooting, trapping, poaching, egg-collecting and animal trading, it is the indirect dangers to their lives that require our immediate concern and attention. On the Queen Charlottes, these dangers include toxic chemicals and the introduction of exotic animals. But the single human activity that seriously threatens birds of prey is the cutting down of mature forests.

Mature trees (mostly spruce) along the coastal fringes of the Queen Charlottes support most of the islands' nesting eagles, falcons and hawks. This critical habitat provides hunting, nesting and maintenance perches for these birds. Studies from other coastal areas tell us that some birds of prey cling tenaciously to their nesting sites, and if these are disturbed or lost, the displaced birds have difficulty renesting.

The dangers pesticides pose to the environment have been well publicized; we are all aware, for example, that DDT has a wide range of adverse effects on wildlife. Top-level predators such as raptors are hit hardest. This form of chemical pollution is global, and the Queen Charlottes has not been spared. Unexpectedly high concentrations of DDT residues have already been found in seabirds, the prey base for most raptors.

Another concern is the aerial spraying of forests to control insect outbreaks. In 1964, parts of the Queen Charlotte Islands were sprayed with phos-

As a top-level carnivore, the bald eagle feeds on the full spectrum of the food chain from snails to fish to large mammals. The accumulative effects of toxic chemicals and the loss of habitat by logging are the greatest threats facing Queen Charlotte Island eagles today.

phamidon, a replacement for DDT, to control the green-striped forest looper. The application was three times the recommended dosage; afterwards, sick and dead forest birds were found in the sprayed areas. What is not known is how the spraying affected other endemic forms of birds, particularly the Steller's jay and hairy woodpecker.

The comparative isolation of the Queen Charlottes serves as some protection for the island raptors and their prey. Human disturbance is far less than in more populated areas, but the risk to predators and prey from the introduction of alien animals, such as minks, foxes and ferrets, is still great. Of course, large-scale logging could quickly destroy much of the habitat now enjoyed by Queen Charlottes' raptors.

People living on the Charlottes have the unique opportunity to prove that, despite what history has shown elsewhere, human occupation of large islands does not have to lead to the eventual demise of its fauna. Those who live close to wild nature probably best appreciate and understand the words of Raymond Gasmann: "Man depends on wildlife for survival, and wildlife depends equally on Man. The two must find means for living together on planet Earth or there will be no life on earth."

117

Very Like a Micro-circuit, 1980—Jim Willer

PART III

THE MOVEMENT

ISLANDS AT THE EDGE

WE HAVE AN INSATIABLE APPETITE FOR TREES, an age-old pattern that stretches back to the dawn of time. Wood and the numberless things we make of it are so much a part of us that it is impossible to imagine a life without it. Perhaps the only thing equal to the extent of our interdependence with trees is the extent to which we take them for granted.

Deep in the forest, a tree's roots sink into the earth and absorb mineral salts which are siphoned into the forest canopy above. In exchange for sustenance, an intricate web of roots imparts stability to the soil. Within the canopy, sunlight penetrates the leaves and fires the photosynthesis of living matter, releasing the oxygen we breathe and live by. The mature forest is a major force in influencing atmospheric humidity and weather patterns, moving and storing huge quantities of water. In one day a large tree can lift a hundred gallons of water out of the ground and discharge it into the air. In exchange for cosmic energy, trees provide most of the earth's creatures with oxygen, water, food, heat and shelter — and they have been doing this for a very long time.

Trees are a powerful lesson in relating to the earth in a way we seem to have forgotten. With roots in the earth and branches in heaven, trees are an archetypal life form, the arc across which life's energies travel, wedding earth and heaven in a dynamic, sustaining relationship. It is a relationship of give and take, an exchange of mutual benefits, which results in a slow but steady accumulation of the most profound kind of wealth — the creation of living matter. Maybe our inability to hear the tree's message is

Trees are conveyors, movers, transmitters — the pathways along which life's energies are exchanged but never lost.

121

self-induced, for ours is a record of alienation from the earth, not relationship . . . of diminishing its wealth, not adding to it.

The multitude of ways in which trees serve us is all-pervasive. Yet whether a tree is shredded and mashed into newsprint or left standing in the forest, there is a common denominator that runs through all of its functions. Trees are conveyors, movers, transmitters, the pathways along which life's energies are changed but never lost.

Even after a tree has been cut, floated to the mill, sawn, chipped, boiled, bent and glued, this theme of transit still remains. The first wheel was fashioned from wood, probably inspired by a rolling log. Wood carried us through the horse and buggy era, and the machines that brought us into the industrial age were cast from patterns made of wood. We build dugout canoes and ocean-going cruisers, make railroad ties, snowshoes, skis, and crutches. We sit on wood and converse with each other, eat from wooden tables, sleep on wooden beds and shelter our families in wooden homes. We rock our babies in wooden cradles and bury our dead in wooden coffins, marking the spot with a wooden cross. We caress wood for comfort, knock on wood for divine insurance, and carve ideas into wood, creating objects of cultural pride.

We beat wood and boil it in acid, rendering its basic fibres into a pulp from which we make all manner of bags and boxes for moving things about. Our exchange of goods and services and our monetary system depends completely on trading bits of paper. With wood cellulose we make film to photograph ourselves, fabrics to clothe our bodies and toilet products to remove our wastes. Newspapers, letters, magazines, posters and books convey our thoughts to ever-widening audiences. We call it the Information Explosion — yet no matter how many headlines the plastic micro-chip miracles are grabbing, those headlines are printed on paper made from trees. Against all expectations, electronic data processing has dramatically increased our use of paper products.

Whether siphoning molecules of water or transporting bits of information on a printed page, the stuff of trees conducts the commerce of life. Yet by all accounts, the world's great forests are in a state of crisis. How could we take such an essential and all-encompassing element so much for granted, to the point that we have obliterated so many of the planet's forests?

PATTERNS OF ABUSE. Problems associated with timber harvesting are occurring the world over. Every region, province, state, country and continent lends its scenario to the planetary picture of abuse. In 1984, trees are being felled throughout the world at a rate of *fifty acres per minute*. In the past thirty years we have cut over one half of the earth's forests. The deforestation of the past seventy-five years has resulted in the loss through erosion of an estimated seventy-five billion tons of topsoil.

The implications of this loss of habitat to the creatures who depend upon it are even more staggering: if present trends continue, by the year 2000 well over 500,000 species will be gone. Within sight is the destruction of plants and animals on a scale that dwarfs the combined natural and human-caused extinctions of the previous millions of years.

In the past thirty years we have cut over one-half of the earth's forests.

The fabric of life is not just suffering a minor tear in a few isolated places — whole sections of it are being ripped apart.

Every government administering the harvest of forests faces the temptation to convert them quickly into valuable foreign exchange. There is usually far greater political appeal to pursuing short-term economic gains than there is to establishing the long-term costs of ecologically reckless consumption patterns and modifying the rate of harvest accordingly.

British Columbia, for instance, has long been blessed with vast stands of mature coniferous forests, enabling us within the past century to build a reputation as a major dealer in the world's wood resources. No country in the world even comes close to matching British Columbia's softwood lumber exports. What is not so widely known is the price exacted from our natural heritage to attain this status.

The industrial history of British Columbia is important to keep in mind when trying to understand the consequences we face today. In the late nineteenth century, having exhausted the easy supplies of gold and fur-bearing animals, the Crown's loyal subjects were staging a mass exodus to less harsh climates. Faced with this alarming loss of taxpayers and labourers — so terribly necessary when one wishes to drain the swamps and build the corridors of power — colonial administrators had to act quickly. The only industrial base remaining was trees and fish, but those were the days when forests were infinite and you walked across streams on the backs of fish. Entrepreneurs had little reason to venture into the hinterlands of Canada when these same resources existed so close to markets farther south.

So reasons were created for them. In principle, the Colony simply gave away its resources on irresistible terms, granting what turned out to be perpetual rights of harvest, often sweetening the pot with outright title to huge tracts of land. The awkward matter of aboriginal ownership of the land being given away was swept under the carpets of the federal government in Ottawa (where it remains to this day) and the pattern was set for the logging industry in British Columbia.

The legacy of this hundred-year habit of catering to industry is now upon us. In British Columbia some 120,000 hectares of mature forest land are cut every year, while only 50,000 are replanted, not all of them successfully. Although forest regeneration occurs naturally on some of the remainder, the total area of land not satisfactorily restocked is over 1,200,000 hectares and growing annually. This was all once prime timber growing land, now lying derelict, stripped of its protection from the erosive forces of wind, sun and water.

The biological impoverishment and squandered economic opportunity that we have inherited brings home a hard lesson: we are far more deeply enmeshed in ecological webs than we think, and the consequences to society of upsetting the stability of the environment are substantial. In fact, incidents of flooding and landslides downstream from logging operations are occurring throughout the province with growing frequency, resulting in tragic losses of fish and wildlife habitat, forest land, private property and occasionally even human life.

The economic consequences of overexploitation are equally disturbing. As our supply of valuable mature wood diminishes, so also does our advantage in the international marketplace, which is full of lower-grade second-growth forest products supplied by far more efficient harvesting and processing

The legacy of this hundred-year habit of catering to industry: whole sections of the fabric of life are being torn apart. (Powrivco Bay, Lyell Island)

technologies from other countries. Following the pattern of the fur trade and the gold rush, forestry has become British Columbia's latest sunset industry.

Nobody is prepared to take responsibility for this loss, although there are plenty of theories about who should. The public, having seen their old-growth forests disappear, maintain that if an industry gains by the removal of a public resource, then surely some of the profits must be returned to the land which provided them. The forest industry, which has beguiled the public for decades with deceptive promises of "sustained yield harvesting" and "multiple resource use," now say it is the public's fault for failing to recognize the trend and demanding that it be corrected by elected officials. The government, finding it politically undesirable to even acknowledge what lies around the corner, has diverted the pathetically small amount of revenues earmarked for silvicultural programs into dam-building, coal mining, high tech and anything else that offers to replace the withering forest cash crop.

THE RPF EFFECT. The pattern of logging on the Queen Charlotte Islands is arguably the best example of overexploitation in all of British Columbia. Certainly some of the province's most infamous examples of habitat destruction caused by logging have occurred on the Charlottes. (Recent studies there show six times as many landslides on logged sites as on natural sites.) Equally outstanding is the cutting of the Islands' forests far in excess of their ability to grow trees on a sustained yield basis. Overseeing this state of affairs is a group of professional resource managers — the Registered Professional Foresters (RPF) — granted standing only after years of rigourous indoctrination in British Columbia forest management methods.

RPFs are day-to-day forest managers, occupying positions of planning and administration in government and industry. They analyze the forest resource and decide on the time and manner of its dispensation. It is a highly technical field, full of long-winded attempts to explain how trees conform to complex computer models. In effect, it is the profession responsible for maximizing the cut (over the short term only) and providing rationalizations for doing so.

Just about every stick of merchantable wood on the Queen Charlottes is slated for harvest. The provincial Forest Service manages this arrangement by dispensing cutting rights under several licensing schemes. One of these is a system called the Timber Supply Area (TSA), through which smaller companies and individual operators acquire one-time rights to harvest trees. The arrangement carries no obligations to care for the land upon which the trees grow. These areas used to be called "Public Sustained Yield Units," a misnomer if ever there was one.

In 1982 the Forest Service released a report on the state of the Queen Charlotte TSA which revealed a rate of logging so blatantly unsustainable that it astonished even the small logging operators and local conservationists, who are normally cynical under the best of circumstances. It began by showing that the land could grow trees at a rate of about 233,000 cubic metres per year. It continued by revealing that the level of harvest was about 583,680 cubic metres

Just about every stick of merchantable wood on the Queen Charlottes is slated for harvest. The economic and environmental consequences will be felt by generations to come.

127

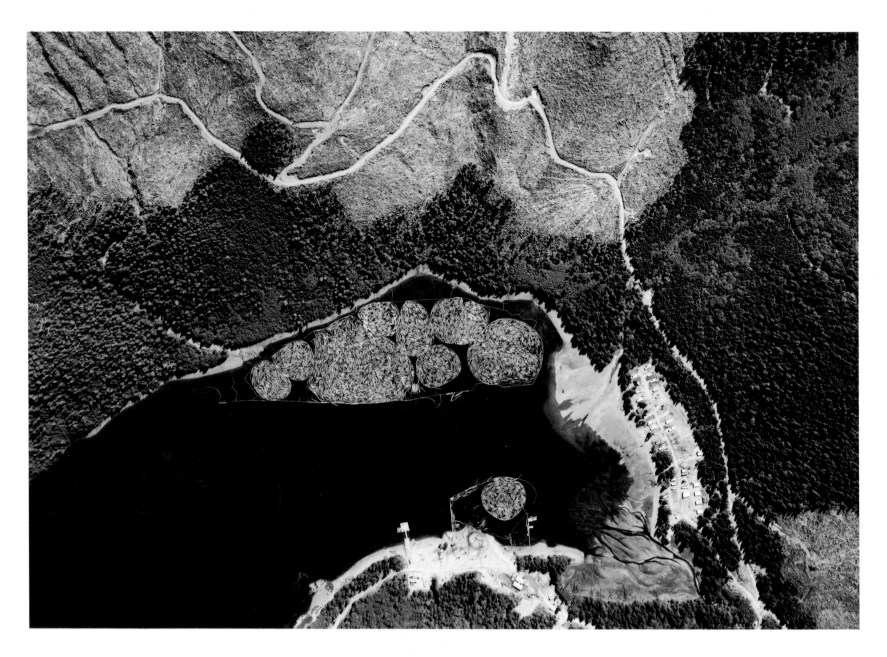

per year. It ended with a glossary that vaguely re-defined Sustained Yield Forestry as "the management of forests so as to achieve continuous production of forest products indefinitely." Contrast this "doublespeak" with the very specific intention of the original concept: for every cubic metre of wood harvested, another one is supposed to be growing to take its place.

Another new definition in the glossary, likewise made necessary by the embarassment of having created a 150-percent overcommitment of the public forest, was Falldown Effect. Simply described, a hectare of old-growth forest contains more cubic metres of wood than a second-growth forest, and we are removing the old-growth forests at a rate far beyond the capacity of the land to replace them. The resulting effect upon the charts and graphs of the forest managers is an abruptly falling line, representing a shortfall in wood supplies of over 60 percent within the next few decades. With the RPF's penchant for wrapping their shortcomings in unintelligible jargon, they call this drop the Falldown Effect.

There are other ways of making the situation appear less desperate than it is, the simplest being to juggle the numbers, and there are lots of numbers to juggle. The obvious place to begin is with timber supply, and the object of the game is to make it look as if there are more trees than those embarrassing headlines say there are. So the Forest Service starts by getting a large, sophisticated computer and creating data processing programs with snappy names like Timber RAM (Resource Analysis Method) and MUSYC (Multiple Use Sustained Yield Calculation). They then annex over 80 percent of the province into a system called the Provincial Forest. It matters little that much of the new bureaucratic empire consists of islands and mountain tops with scrubby little trees of no commercial value. Those trees are numbers for the computer, and numbers add up.

The next step in manipulating the database is called "intensive silviculture." Through such techniques as juvenile spacing, fertilization and genetic tree improvement programs, theoretical second-growth yields increase up to 300 percent over actual regeneration levels.

Having thus amassed a large number of cubic metres of indeterminate validity, the other key figure to juggle is how long it takes to grow a new crop of trees. This has been accomplished by redefining a "mature" tree, from one of three hundred years or so downwards to a hundred and twenty . . . ninety . . . eighty . . . even sixty years. It doesn't matter that a tree will not even begin to grow the long, tough, commercially valuable fibres until after its first century.

Where landslides or roads have scarred the land, prompting colonization by nitrogen-fixing alders, "rehabilitation" with chemicals eliminates the thirty-year delay required for natural succession by conifers. The object of this exercise is to take all the wood that has been "found" or planned for growing and divide it by a conveniently short "rotation age." On paper then, the wood supply problem disappears, and forest managers can justify levels of harvest on the grounds that there is plenty of wood.

But of course there isn't. There are no funds for intensive silviculture programs; they were diverted long ago by a government more intent on political images than responsible resource husbandry. The

Far from creating long-term economic and social stability, logging methods in British Columbia reflect a gold-rush mentality towards the forests. The attitude is so deeply ingrained that even while South Moresby was being studied for park protection, logging continued over the northern quarter of the original wilderness proposal. (Powrivco Camp, Lyell Island)

The proposal, in 1974, by the company logging TFL #24 to move from Talunkwan Island (above) south to Burnaby Narrows caused understandable alarm. One decade later, the "Talunkwanization" of South Moresby has spread south over Lyell Island (opposite) to the edge of Juan Perez Sound (visible at extreme left).

province does not even grow enough seedlings to meet the replanting requirements of basic silviculture. And those gnarled cedar and pine trees along the seashore and in the alpine areas will never really be harvested.

The only advantage British Columbia ever had in international lumber markets — the superior fibre characteristics of old-growth wood — will disappear when we begin to cut sixty-year-old trees. The whole absurd exercise has been conducted simply to buy time, to increase the allocation of the last few remaining stands of mature forest to be cut as soon as possible and processed by outdated, inefficient, wasteful technologies. Instead of alleviating the falldown effect and its enormous economic and ecological consequences, the forestry profession has precipitated its earlier arrival.

GOVERNMENT BY OUTRAGE. In October of 1974 ITT-Rayonier Canada (B.C.) Ltd., the holder of Tree Farm Licence #24, presented a five-year logging plan which proposed to move their contractor logging operation south from Talunkwan Island to Burnaby Island. They could not have left behind a more ecologically devastated area. Talunkwan Island, with its massive clearcuts over unstable slopes, is known even to foresters as the worst environmental horror show in British Columbia. Ravaged by landslides with every rainy season, the spectre of Talunkwan is a constantly renewing indictment of forestry practices on the Charlottes.

The Skidegate Band Council, whose members hold strong ancestral ties to South Moresby, objected to the plan because they rely on the area for sustenance, as well as cultural and spiritual inspira-

tion. They felt that the logging plans would degrade the quality of the land and thus the quality of their lives. The Haida maintain hereditary ownership of the Queen Charlottes and have never surrendered their lands or entered into a treaty with Canada or the province.

At the same time the general public voiced its concerns through the newly formed Islands Protection Committee (later to become the Islands Protection Society). A proposal to preserve the area south of the Tangil Peninsula as a wilderness area was drafted and submitted to the provincial government. In November the parties to the conflict met in Skidegate with government agencies, resulting in a decision to defer the plan to log Burnaby Island. The company then applied for approval to log on Lyell Island in the northern part of the Wilderness Proposal, and four months later was granted permission to proceed.

In February of 1975 a petition bearing the signatures of five hundred Island residents was delivered to the Provincial Legislature. It requested a moratorium on *all* logging within the South Moresby Wilderness Proposal area until environmental impact studies could be completed. Concerns were expressed over increasing instances of slope failure and damage to salmonid spawning habitat on the Queen Charlottes and especially within TFL #24 itself on Talunkwan Island. As a result, in April of 1975 the Environment and Land Use Committee (ELUC) of the provincial cabinet instructed its Secretariat to prepare an overview study of the wilderness proposal.

In July of 1976, Secretariat staff toured South Moresby and consulted with various interested parties and the public. Over the next year studies were

conducted by the provincial Parks Branch for park potential; by the Forest Ministry for "environmental protection area" assessment; by the Ministry of Environment and the Provincial Museum for seabird, raptor, mammal and freshwater fish inventories; by the Ecological Reserves Unit for potential ecological reserve requirements, and by the Ministry of Energy, Mines and Petroleum Resources for mineral potential.

During the same period Parks Canada commissioned a study of the area's natural history in order to assess its potential for National Park status and declared it a "Natural Area of Canadian Significance." At the south end of the Charlottes, Anthony Island was in the process of nomination as a UNESCO World Heritage Cultural Site, implemented in 1982.

The South Moresby Wilderness Proposal began at the grassroots level, as do all environmental conservation issues. Political leaders rarely possess enough appreciation of biological diversity to support the conservation of an area — and so those who do are faced with the formidable task of countering the pressures to exploit it as well as inspiring government into action. Unwittingly, the forest industry itself helped a great deal to change the minds of those who were initially reluctant to lend their support, by harvesting without restraint close to the major population centres. Watching their surroundings deteriorate into one huge clearcut landscape within the space of a decade, local residents came to a first-hand appreciation of conservation issues. In January of 1976, the first major article about South Moresby to appear in a national periodical was published in *Nature Canada,* the journal of the Canadian Nature Federation.

In November of 1977, the extent of public awareness increased with the Second All-Islands Symposium, a popular forum for local self-determination issues, sponsored by IPS on the topic of "Resource Conflict in the South Moresby Wilderness Proposal." Attended by representatives from industry, federal and provincial government agencies and numerous public interest organizations, the two-day event resulted in a resolution calling for public hearings into the renewal of TFL #24. This was heralded as an appropriate opportunity to examine ITT-Rayonier's track record before allowing it another twenty-five year tenure.

The year 1978 brought increasing attention to South Moresby by the media, the general public and elected representatives. Following major film and television programs, formal endorsements of the wilderness proposal began to appear from public groups such as the Nature Federations of B.C., Alberta and Saskatchewan, and also from special interest groups, such as the Pacific Seabird Group, representing biologists from thiry-nine countries, who wished to prevent further destruction of critical seabird nesting habitat. This trend has ultimately brought support from hundreds of organizations across Canada, ranging in interests from the Nature Federation of Canada to the Travel Industry Association of Canada, and representing at last count well over 300,000 people.

In January, the proposal to establish an ecological reserve on Lyell Island over the Dodge Point Murrelet colony and the Windy Bay watershed was confirmed, creating further conflicts with logging interests in South Moresby. In May, the new British Columbia Forest Act was introduced in the Legislature, providing for automatic renewal of Tree Farm

The mature forest is a major force in influencing atmospheric humidity and weather patterns as it moves and stores huge quantities of water.

Licences, without public hearings as requested in several areas of the province. In June, in spite of widespread opposition, the Forest Act was rushed through third and fourth readings, leaving the matter of hearings to the Minister's discretion.

TAKING THE MINISTER TO COURT. By the end of the year it was apparent that the changes required to conserve South Moresby would not be easily won. The Graham Island Advisory Planning Committee, MP Iona Campagnolo, MLA Graham Lea and a long list of other public groups had called upon the Minister for TFL #24 renewal hearings. So too had the Forest Service's own Public Advisory Committee.

In January 1979 the Islands Protection Society, Nathan Young (the hereditary chief of Tanoo and a native trapper in South Moresby), Gary Edenshaw (representing Haida hunter-gatherers) and Glenn Naylor (holder of a registered trapline on Burnaby Island) filed a joint petition in the Supreme Court of British Columbia, asking for a ruling which would ensure that their interests were fairly considered by the Minister. Evidence was presented which showed that trapping and food-gathering were impaired by logging practices, and most notably that the government was permitting harvesting activities in violation of its own guidelines. The petitioners' allegations, which were not contested, included harvesting too quickly to maintain "sustained yield," cutting on unstable slopes too sensitive to withstand erosion and landslides and damaging salmonid spawning streams. In a precedent-setting decision, the judge granted standing to all of the petitioners except IPS, and ruled that the Minister of Forests was under a duty to act fairly and allow them to examine and respond to all information used to reach a decision on the renewal of TFL #24.

Three months later the ELUC Secretariat released its long-awaited Overview Study, which called for a five-year study of multiple resource use options. The report appeared to have been a last-minute rush to provide back-up for the government's defense in the court case and contained many inaccuracies. By April, the petitioners still had not been able to obtain any information from the Minister and so returned to court. Pleading forgetfulness, the Forest Ministry invited them to a meeting at which they were asked to drop the latest action, coming as it did in the midst of a provincial election campaign. The petitioners responded with fifteen proposed changes to the terms of TFL #24. During the negotiations that followed, they elicited a surprising admission that sustained yield forestry has never actually been practised in B.C. They also discovered that the Minister had received sixty submissions from individuals and organizations (representing some 200,000 people) in favour of renewal hearings and only three opposed — the opposite of the Ministry's public statements to the press. In the end, the Deputy Minister agreed to make six changes to the TFL agreement and attempted once more to have the legal action dropped. The petitioners chose to return to court. Two days before the renewal of TFL #24, the petition was dismissed on the grounds that the Minister had still not yet renewed the licence, and by all appearances was prepared to make changes which demonstrated his intentions to act fairly.

In May TFL #24 was renewed for another twenty-five years *without* the promised changes, and the Social Credit party was elected to a new term of

office. The petitioners initiated a third court action, eventually heard in January of 1980.

In the meantime, the Forest Service called the first meeting of the South Moresby Resource Planning Team, drawing together representatives of the Skidegate Band Council, IPS, Rayonier, the Queen Charlotte Islands Museum Society, the Forest Service, the Ministry of Environment, the Lands Branch, the Parks Branch, Mines, the Ecological Reserves Unit, Federal Fisheries and a member of the Public Advisory Committee to the Forest Service. Touted as a model of the new public involvement process, it was to be "a decision-making team, with substantial authority delegated from the Forest Service and other agencies." It was obvious at the

The ratio of landslides in logged to unlogged watersheds is six to one. Landslides cause extensive damage to Queen Charlotte salmonid habitat. Opposite: spawning pink salmon in Windy Bay creek. Above: landslide in creek drainage on Louise Island.

outset that this would prove to be a hollow mandate — when the Forest Service carefully set terms of reference which precluded any possibility of establishing the original wilderness proposal.

In September the Public Advisory Committee, doomed to failure by a nebulous mandate and the refusal of the Ministry of Forests to provide access to the resource data required for meaningful analysis, voted to disband itself. It was perhaps the only recommendation that the Forest Service accepted without hesitation from its own awkward experiment in public involvement.

In October of that year, continuous heavy rainfall brought landslides, washouts, flooding and heavy damages to clearcut watersheds throughout northern B.C. and the Queen Charlotte Islands. Hundreds of landslides occurred on the Charlottes, many of them at Rennell Sound on the west coast of Graham Island, including the infamous Riley Creek. Earlier in 1979 the federal Department of Fisheries and Oceans and the provincial Ministry of Environment had halted logging on unstable slopes above Riley Creek, a productive salmon spawning stream. The company ignored a federal order to cease cutting; charges were laid under the Fisheries Act of Canada and eventually dropped after a long and heated debate involving the two governments, the International Woodworkers of America labour union and some of the larger logging companies.

IPS sponsored yet another court petition, this time citing the senior federal and provincial officials who had negotiated the dropping of charges, the resumption of logging — and the resulting destruction of millions of pink salmon fry. But these charges were stayed by the provincial Attorney-General without explanation, before ever having reached court.

In January of 1980 the petitioners in the TFL #24 case returned to court and were dismissed, primarily on the grounds that the Minister had already made his decision. The single concession granted was a ruling that the petitioners could have access to the Management and Working Plans for TFL #24 before approval was given and that they would be allowed to make substantial comment. But, despite a professionally prepared demonstration that a slower rate and different pattern of cut were required if the Ministry's own guidelines for environmental protection were to be applied, when the allowable annual cut was announced, it showed a reduction of less than one percent. The case was ultimately taken to the Supreme Court of Canada, where it was denied leave to appeal on the grounds that it was a provincial matter.

THE SOUTH MORESBY RESOURCE PLANNING TEAM. From the outset, the team's supposed mandate of "substantial authority delegated from the Forest Service and other agencies" was a farce. The Forest Ministry continued its pattern from the old Public Advisory Committee days of dragging its heels over requests for meaningful resource information. Field research requirements were dismissed as fiscally impossible. The Ministry of Mines was quick to throw its own wrench into the works, refusing outright the team's repeated requests for a temporary reserve on claim-staking until the report was completed. This eventually resulted in the ecological reserve proposal area at Windy Bay being

Black bear beside stream. Forests provide most of earth's creatures with oxygen, water, food, heat and shelter.

covered by mineral claims of no apparent value other than to make the establishment of ecological reserve status a legal impossibility.

The same pattern was repeated in the matter of the team's mandate as a "decision-maker." In late 1983, when the team's final report was approaching completion, it was decided, in keeping with the original Forest Ministry policy, that "a draft final plan should be presented at a public event, to allow for review by interested parties who, for practical reasons, could not sit in on the working group." This was not to be.

After members had met for four years, visited the area, examined its various resources and attempted to evaluate them, South Moresby was beginning to grow on the team. It was becoming obvious that the majority favoured conservation, and loud complaints arose from industry that the team had an "environmentalist bent." Then the word filtered down through the bureaucracy: there would be no public meetings, the report would contain no concensus recommendation on the area's allocation and government agency members were to refrain from expressing their views on this matter in public. For the public members of the planning team, it was the crowning lesson in cynicism.

South Moresby was not the only conservation issue to be dealt with by the government's multiple resource use planning team approach, and not the only public involvement exercise to reach the same conclusions. Over the years that the South Moresby team was meeting, other reports were received by the government and ultimately ignored to greater or lesser degrees. In the minds of its participants, "public involvement" degenerated in concept from a

meaningful democratic exercise to a clever diversion by government of conservationist energies and a measure for avoiding embarassing legal confrontations.

The result of the whole exercise is a predictably bland document, a product of writing by committee. It is in the end little more than a cost-benefit analysis, containing all of the classic pitfalls of its genre. The resource industries, inventors of the cost-benefit game, deal in "tangible values": neat columns of numbers — cubic metres of wood, metric tonnes of mineral possibilities, billions of dollars, thousands of man-hours. The conservationists counter with the "intangible values" — bird colonies, archaeological sites, scientific research, spiritual communion, wilderness recreation. It is a primitive tool of analysis, incapable of weighing the real issue at stake, and one of the report's few redeeming features is that it says as much.

And so the ball returns to the Environment and Land Use Committee of the provincial cabinet. The planning team report has presented them with four "options," representing varying degrees of industrial intrusion or wilderness preservation in South Moresby. Each option has a price tag listing dollars, birds and kilometres of shoreline. Recently, some honourable members were heard to complain about the lack of substance in the report. But it was their own minions who scrupulously ensured that it contains no potentially compromising recommendations, leaving themselves with nothing to react to, nothing to reject and nothing to confirm.

Yet the five-year term of the planning team was not without its benefits. Foremost among these was the delay factor, which allowed for five years of

Darwin Sound in the north end of the South Moresby wilderness proposal.

organizing and gathering support. Attracted by the area's growing reputation as a rare cultural and wilderness experience, a tourism industry has developed virtually overnight. With the exposure of writers, photographers, artists and scientists to the area, word of its particular value and the efforts to conserve it have spread to an international audience.

The five-year term was also not without serious drawbacks for South Moresby itself, such as the sacrificing of the northern quarter of the original wilderness proposal by extensive clearcut logging on Lyell Island, and also the staking of mineral claims over much of South Moresby. The original proposal to issue a moratorium on all development until a decision could be made — a seemingly logical approach to take — was never honoured by the government of British Columbia.

Touch the earth. Somewhere in our distant past we chose the company of man over the company of the earth, the urban over the rural. We are fascinated by ourselves more than any other form of life, and we have replaced the old graven images with mirrors. Where once we looked to Mother Earth for succour, now we look to the city. This massive cultural introversion has transformed not only our way of relating to the earth, but also the earth itself.

What have we achieved in all this? What are the telltale effects upon our collective spirit? Well, we seem to live a life tinged slightly with panic, full of deadlines and headlines. We rush through a life full of days too short, until we suffer breakdowns of one sort or another. We are afraid of many things. And like the missionaries of old we spread our lifestyle throughout the world, converting commies with bluejeans and mass-marketing pop stars in third world ghettos. We are so preoccupied by the clamour and glamour of our throw-away culture that we rarely notice when something has gone wrong until it reaches crisis proportions.

Well, a crisis is upon us. Our lifestyle has exacted a huge price from the environment, one that we have been blithely willing to pay only because we have never really known its extent.

Not many of us would draw a connection between a nuclear warhead and an endangered butterfly in Costa Rica or a clearcut watershed on the Queen Charlotte Islands. It is time to do so. Each folly is a consequence of our untenable attitude toward the earth — the wisdom of the tree eludes us. We take uranium from deep in the earth and with clever technology harness its power to our own self-indulgent ends. In effect we would destroy the earth in defence of the right to exploit it. We are smart but not wise. The closest we come to treating the earth as kin is as if it were a rich relative, taking more and still more from it without any notion of gratitude, never caring to give anything in return.

We are a civilization out of balance, and correcting this condition is the great challenge of our age. Hopefully the environmental and spiritual crisis that we have precipitated is provoking us into the awareness that we require, for we have just about reached the limits of our alienation. Those among us who lived here long before, who lived another way, who listened for the messages of trees, have this to say:

You must teach your children that the ground beneath their feet is the ashes of our

Mortuary pole with bear and human, Ninstints World Heritage Site.

Morning kayakers in Mitchell Inlet. The earth does not belong to man, man belongs to the earth.

grandfathers. So that they will respect the land, tell your children that the earth is rich with the lives of our kin. Teach your children what we have taught our children, that the earth is our mother. Whatever befalls the earth befalls the sons and daughters of the earth. If men spit upon the ground, they spit upon themselves.

This we know: the earth does not belong to man, man belongs to the earth. This we know. All things are connected like the blood that unites one family. All things are connected. Man did not weave the web of life, he is merely a strand in it. Whatever he does to the web, he does to himself.

Whatever befalls the earth befalls the sons and daughters of the earth.

Chief Sealth of the Duamish tribe

The call to preserve places such as South Moresby signals a new tradition of land use, or rather the adoption of an ancient one. And while such timeless wisdom as Sealth's will not be easy for some of us to swallow, it is far more palatable than the alternative. No doubt, the conservation of South Moresby will have an influence on many other land use issues, including, we hope, the end of "multiple use" abuse.

It is fitting that the great conservation struggles are focussing on the forests, because preserving them does more than just protect natural habitat. The very act requires that we collectively embrace that other ethic of land use, that we consciously choose to become truly North American, to sink our roots deep into this Mother Earth, to finally come home.

VISITORS WHO DO NOT REMAIN

Few places in the world offer a wilderness experience as rich and varied as the south end of the Queen Charlotte archipelago. Indeed, it is difficult to imagine any place on earth with a comparable expanse of geographical, cultural, scenic, biological and recreational features. Those who have been fortunate enough to experience South Moresby first-hand have discovered a wilderness in the classical sense: a place where the earth and its community of life are untrammelled by man. Whether future visitors will enjoy a pristine wilderness will depend not only on the conservation of the area from industrial development but also on its wise management as a park.

One of the problems of popularizing a wilderness area like South Moresby in order to conserve it is the possibility of attracting too many visitors, thus endangering the wilderness characteristics for which protection was originally sought. In the past few years first-hand knowledge of the special features of South Moresby has spread far beyond local residents and the academic institutions and government agencies who have sent field research teams to the area. As the network of support for conserving the area has grown, so too has interest in its wilderness recreation opportunities.

From 1978 to 1982 the number of visitors to South Moresby on organized commercial tours increased eleven-fold. Most of these tours have been by special interest groups from across Canada, the United States and Europe, including parks associations, museum and naturalist societies, art galleries, schools and ethnography associations. In addition, the numbers of private individuals who visit the area

The peace and tranquillity of the South Moresby experience can be every bit as fragile as the wilderness itself.

145

Hikers in the San Cristoval Range.
Recreational users are finding their way to South
Moresby in increasing numbers.

by coastal cruiser, or who take advantage of the recently introduced provincial ferry service to the Charlottes, has also increased dramatically.

At present, with no legislation to curtail logging and mining development and no official park status to safeguard against visitor abuse, South Moresby is suffering the impact of both. It is not enough to say that the wilderness recreation industry is a lesser evil than resource extraction, and allow it to develop without plan. There are too many extremely fragile features that can be altered or destroyed by overuse or ignorance, however sensitive or well-intentioned visitors may be.

Fortunately, it is not necessary to rely on trial and error in developing management strategies for visitors to ecologically fragile areas. There are a number of parks and preserves throughout the world that are already dealing with similar problems, some quite successfully. One of the best examples of successful management is an area to which South Moresby has already been compared — the Galapagos Islands.

THE GALAPAGOS REVISITED. Lying astride the equator about eight hundred kilometres off South America's Pacific coast, the Galapagos Islands are, in biological terms, unlike any other place in the world. Over 80 percent of the animal species found there are endemic. When these remote volcanic isles were visited by Charles Darwin in 1835, they acted as the catalyst that inspired his theory of evolution. In 1859 Darwin published *The Origin of the Species* and generated a revolution in thought which completely altered man's way of seeing himself. Exactly one hundred years later the Galapagos were declared a national park, and an international panel of scientists was convened to devise a system of management that would safeguard the islands' unique flora and fauna.

Today, a carefully controlled twelve thousand visitors per year converge on the Galapagos from all corners of the globe to marvel at the amazing diversity and abundance of wildlife. As these islands never supported populations of aboriginal man, and as most of the wildlife display no instinctive fear of man, one would think that such a recent deluge of humans would have severe impact. Such is not the case. Most of the havoc here was brought about by exotic species (goats, pigs and rats) introduced by buccaneers, whalers and settlers long before the national park was created. Since that time a massive educational/public relations program has been launched by the park service to fully inform local residents of park goals and to solicit their co-operation in its preservation.

Some of the regulations governing the Galapagos National Park may seem extreme by North American standards. For instance, no private yachts or vessels are allowed to visit the many islands without an official Parks guide. Some islands are completely off limits to visitor use, others are of such an undisturbed nature that, before going ashore, guides actually check visitors' pant cuffs for attached seeds lest a new exotic plant be unintentionally introduced.

Certainly the concern for the accidental or deliberate introduction of new species should be a paramount concern on South Moresby. The region's endemic species are most susceptible to disturbance by introduced species. Deer, beaver, rat, raccoon and other species introduced to the Charlottes have already had major impact. The 1977 introduction of domestic goats to Ramsay Island was a thoughtless

146

act on the part of some temporary "back to the land" people that may yet have major consequences for other South Moresby islands. In 1957 a Galapagos fisherman introduced three goats to Pinta Island, and within ten years they had produced fourteen thousand offspring. A feral goat eradication program on Hood Island in the Galapagos (smaller in size than Ramsey) required hundreds of hunters and cost hundreds of thousands of dollars before the unwanted animals were eliminated. On larger, more rugged islands, both on the Charlottes and the Galapagos, the task would be nearly impossible. Moreover, household pets such as dogs and cats should not be allowed into South Moresby unleashed. A population of feral cats could eradicate a seabird colony in short order.

In addition to controlling the introduction of new species to the islands, the Galapagos National Park has demonstrated considerable success in minimizing the impact of visitors on seabird colonies. Some seabird islands and colonies are strictly off limits to visitors. Those locations where visitors are permitted have carefully marked pathways designed to give a close look at the colony without disturbing actual nest sites. As a further safeguard, all tour groups are personally escorted through these areas by park guides.

Similar strategies will have to be employed in South Moresby for excursions ashore to seabird nesting colonies, most of which are occupied during the peak tourist months. At a time when adult seabirds need all of their resources to raise their young, they can waste valuable energy worrying over curious intruders.

Galapagos National Park has also set an important precedent in protecting its littoral marine zone. A several-kilometer radius around all islands is closed to commercial fishing. Such a move in South Moresby would undoubtedly meet with stiff resistance from Federal Fisheries as well as the fishing industry. Still, there is little value in protecting wildlife habitat from logging, mining and other industrial degradation if an animal is to be deprived of its food source. Most animals in South Moresby depend either directly or indirectly on marine foods. We must not allow the situation which is resulting in massive bird starvation in Atlantic Canada to repeat itself here. All commercial fisheries in South Moresby must be re-evaluated. Quotas must reflect not only the sustained yield capacity of a commercial fish species based on human predation but the priority requirements of resident wildlife populations as well.

One of the great thrills for South Moresby visitors is to approach by boat close to a sea lion haulout or rookery and watch tons of furry flesh cascade over the rocks into the sea. Because of a long history of harassment by fishermen, and an even longer history of predation by aboriginal Haidas, these mammals have a strong instinctive fear of man. When approached by people they invariably panic and head for the safety of the sea. While this is a great spectacle to observe and makes a dramatic display on film, it can be difficult or impossible for the sea lions to regain their perches during low tides. The question remains as to how much of this disturbance these mammals can or should tolerate.

Whales are another marine mammal which may require some protection from visitors. Studies in Alaska's Glacier Bay National Monument (420

Juan Perez Sound viewed from above Hecate Strait. Like the Galapagos Islands, South Moresby will require careful regulations to protect its endemic flora and fauna.

Alarmed by an approaching boat, Steller sea lions plunge to the safety of the sea. Disturbance to haulouts and rookeries is one of the impacts uncontrolled visitor use can have on South Moresby wildlife.

kilometres north of the Queen Charlottes) have demonstrated a dramatic decline of humpback whales over the past decade as the number of cruise ships and pleasure craft increased in their favoured feeding waters. While cause and effect have not been conclusively proven in this case, the U.S. Department of the Interior has taken the precautionary step of restricting boat access to the bay.

There are no known special feeding areas in South Moresby for whales. But recently, with increased visitor use to the area, whale sightings and recordings have increased. Several distinct pods of orcas are thought to be resident in South Moresby waters, though little is known about their behaviour. As more is learned about whales here, it is foreseeable that preferred feeding areas, rubbing beaches or nursery areas may be identified and protected from too much human disturbance.

Raptors are another cause for concern, especially the bird whose name is virtually synonymous with wilderness, the Peale's peregrine falcon — found in South Moresby in the world's largest known concentrations. The sight of these magnificent birds in the wild is one of the greatest experiences wilderness has to offer. Falcon aeries are particularly susceptible to disturbance and are located in extremely inaccessible locations as a strategy against predators. However, skilled rock climbers can, and do, reach these sites. They do so as illegal poachers, or with authorization from the B.C. Fish and Wildlife Branch during a "legal falcon harvest." Both thefts, justified on whatever grounds, are completely incompatible with the wilderness integrity of this area. Falcon aeries, eagle nests and other breeding sites for raptors should remain as free as possible from all human disturbance. If necessary, off-limit

buffer zones should be established around active falcon aeries on a seasonal basis to assure total protection. A similar system of temporary zone closures is employed very successfully in Alaska's Denali National Park and Preserve to protect wolf denning sites from human disturbance during the critical breeding and rearing period.

Another place where zone closures are effectively used in Denali is in protecting visitors from unusually aggressive grizzlies or areas of high bear concentrations. While the Queen Charlotte black bear is usually timid by nature, it is the world's largest, and could pose problems if harassed at creeks during the salmon spawning season. Again there are many time-proven management systems which allow this spectacle to be viewed by visitors in safety, such as observation towers and naturalist guide escorts.

MAINTAINING THE MYSTIQUE. Just as it is necessary to minimize human disturbance to wildlife, it is also important to protect wilderness visitors from disturbing each other. Certain locations in South Moresby are already experiencing seasonal congestion, most notably Hot Spring Island and the village of Ninstints on *Skun gwai* (Red Cod Island). The peace and solitude of lying in a tub of soothing sulphurs on one's own paradise island, or coming upon the great array of totem poles and haunting silence on the remote shores of *Skun gwai* are now nearly a thing of the past. Of course, the great influx of visitors is still, and is likely to remain, a seasonal phenomenon. Anyone adventurous enough to visit South Moresby in the winter months, or to brave the west coast at any time of the

year, will undoubtedly find the wilderness solitude they seek.

Conflicts have already begun to surface between some of the wide-ranging recreational users. Satisfying the recreational requirements of travellers by kayak, cruise ship, charter fishing vessel, motorized inflatable, private yacht, helicopter and float plane will not be an easy task.

Cruise ships, although they may seem the antithesis of wilderness to many, do allow some people to experience the area who could not otherwise do so. Glacier Bay National Monument in Alaska allows cruise ships but restricts the number permitted to enter. The Galapagos National Park has successfully adopted the same policy although here restrictions are further placed on the number of islands that cruise ships may visit. Similar policies should be employed for the bigger vessels touring South Moresby. Anchorages should be selected which will shield, as much as possible, the visual impact of these "floating hotels." At the same time, small-craft users have a certain obligation not to sprawl their camps along shore in clear view of major boating corridors. Of course the best landing beaches and campsites were discovered and occupied over the past ten thousand years; virtually every good campsite is either a former Haida summer camp or winter village. Again, regulations will be required to protect these sensitive archaeological sites from overuse.

One of the more controversial modes of transport in wilderness settings is aircraft. South Moresby from the air is truly a spectacle to behold, and for some people it is their favoured way of experiencing it. Still, some type of regulations seem in order. Aircraft could conceivably be restricted to certain routes through South Moresby, as well as having controlled points for embarking and disembarking passengers.

Another recreational feature of South Moresby is back-country use. Denali National Park and Preserve in Alaska could serve as a model with its excellent back-country use system. The park is zoned on a map following natural contours. Back-country use permits are issued free of charge at the park headquarters on a first-come first-serve basis. As soon as a certain number of people obtain permits for a specific zone, it is then temporarily closed to new permits. The system is so effective that backpackers almost never encounter other parties, thereby assuring a quality wilderness experience.

WILDERNESS ETIQUETTE. We must never forget that the South Moresby wilderness is the legacy of thousands of years of stewardship by the Haida, and that their cultural identity remains inseparably linked to the land. As a means of safeguarding the area from visitor abuse, the Haida Nation requires all commercial tour operators to obtain a permit and abide by guidelines designed to protect the integrity of the area.

Some of the Haida concerns, as well as those of more and more people, deal with wilderness etiquette. The South Moresby wilderness must be managed on a pack-in pack-out basis. Garbage dumps alter the behaviour of wild bears and breed rats that pose a hazard to ground-nesting sea birds; they must not be permitted under any circumstances. In addition, beachwood fires should not be extravagant, and all fires should be restricted to the beach zone. Standing wood (alive or dead) should remain standing.

Fossil records, agates and Haida artifacts should all remain on location. Beachcombing should be restricted to articles of flotsam and jetsam, leaving the outdoor natural history museum intact.

Finally, there is the question of wild foods utilization. South Moresby is an area of outstanding food resources both for humans and the myriad of animals that inhabit it. Visitors should take no more than what they can eat on location.

ZERO HOUR. By the turn of this century, whatever wilderness remains will be in parks or other managed areas. At the present time only 5 percent of the earth's land area has some type of protected status.

Here in Canada the crisis seems far less urgent than in many countries. We enjoy one of the world's highest standards of living and still retain some options on wilderness preservation. It is becoming increasingly clear, however, that those options are fast disappearing. Alaska has recently designated more lands as National Parks and Preserves than are currently protected in all of Canada. Even many impoverished third-world countries have set aside more parkland than has Canada. For example, Indonesia has set aside 9 percent, the Commonwealth of Dominica 25 percent and Tanzania 26 percent. Compare this with 0.08 percent for Canada.

The challenge of our age is not only the need to conserve more areas of the natural world but also to safeguard those parks already established. Even in

Two visitors to the Bischof Islands find the wilderness solitude they seek. With increasing numbers of visitors to the area, however, uncontrolled tourism may have to give way to a certain level of regulation to protect the quality of that experience.

North America the clamour has begun to get at timber and mineral wealth within existing parks. The gross mismanagement of our natural resources, particularly timber, is the paramount reason why it is so difficult to preserve areas such as South Moresby — even though the timber land in South Moresby represents less than one-tenth of a percent of the productive forest land in B.C.

There are no hard-and-fast, inflexible lines in Nature. Complete ecosystems do not lend themselves to simple enclosures by lines on a map, or all encompassing management strategies. For South Moresby to receive real protection there must be a new land ethic for those areas under industrial resource utilization outside the proposed park. The archaic logging practices evident throughout B.C. now resulting in massive wood waste, loss of topsoil, damage to stream and marine environments, and destruction of wildlife habitat must be challenged and reversed. Only then will the future be guaranteed for a wilderness such as South Moresby, a place where man himself is a visitor who does not remain.

ACKNOWLEDGEMENTS

ANYBODY WHO HAS LIVED on the Queen Charlottes and attended the ceremonies of the Haida people knows that there is an art to acknowledging the assistance given by others to whatever project is being celebrated. Credit is given where it is due, usually in the form of lengthy speech-making, and is witnessed by the community. It is a noble tradition with much to recommend it. Individuals get the chance, quite rightly, to feel good about themselves and about the contributions they've made to a community effort.

The movement to conserve South Moresby has been growing for a decade now, and this book has been in the process of assembly for two of those years, all of which has called for much voluntary effort by many people. It is a pleasure to at last have this opportunity to thank everybody — and there are many to thank.

The scope and intensity of support for this book project has been overwhelming. All of the authors have freely contributed their manuscripts, often the outcome of years of professional study and research, and submitted themselves without complaint to endless editorial intrusions. Each of the contributors — writers, artists and photographers — has foregone all proceeds from sales in favour of their allocation by the Islands Protection Society to the conservation of South Moresby.

For sharing the idea of this book from the beginning and seeing it through two years to completion, first thanks belong to John Broadhead and Thom Henley. Tom Reimchen and Sheila Douglas reviewed manuscripts and made many helpful suggestions. Jim Allen reviewed the chapter on visitor use and provided the insight of years of experience as a professional wilderness tour guide in South Moresby. Doug Cowell and Cameron Young gave invaluable editorial assistance. Gudrun Steinerstauch contributed immeasureably to the book's design. And for his help from the outset, a special thank you is due to Bill Reid.

For assistance in many little ways, and a couple of large ones, particular appreciation goes to Greg Hartnup, Ken Lutes, Martine Reid and Maurice Strong. For start-up funding, the generous assistance of the Canada Employment Program is gratefully acknowledged.

Without the photographers, of course, this book simply would not be. Most have endured long separation from some of their best photographs with gratifying generosity, patience and understanding. Of the fifty thousand or so photographs reviewed for the book, only a hundred and thirty-one could be published. Yet even if a photograph could not be included in the book, many have found their way into the public slide show presentations which have enlisted so much support for the conservation of South Moresby. For their very special role a heartfelt thank you is due to: Art Babcock, Dan Bowditch, Dan Conrad, Rosemarie Culver, Bob Dalgleish, Lindsay Eberts, Brian Eccles, Dennis Fast, Simone Flynn, Larry Hale, Irv Krause, Mary Morris, Wilfried Penker, Tom Reimchen, Paul Reimer, Hans Roemer, Wayne Stetsky, June West and Lorraine Worbey.

Even before the book was conceived, there was a map of the Queen Charlotte Islands. A line was drawn upon it and it was called the South Moresby Wilderness Proposal. Those who drew the line were Guujaw (Gary Edenshaw), Wanagan (Dick Wilson) and Huckleberry (Thom Henley). The dream was quickly adopted by a great many others whose ranks have not ceased to grow, inspired by the power and grace of this small but very special part of the earth.

Some of these people formed the Islands Protection Committee, later to become a Society. Others were allies who shared a common goal, some not necessarily agreeing with all of the things IPS was to do or say, but over the years providing artistic talent, energy, information, money, facilities, letter-writing skills, legal and administrative services, music, potluck dinners, personal connections and an endless stream of commentary and free advice. Among them, in very rough chronological order of dreaming the dream are:

Percy Williams (President of the Haida Nation), Nathan Young (Chief Tanoo), Sam and Jesse Simpson, Howard Phillips, Viola Wood, Sergius de Bucy, Glenn Naylor, Trudy Carson, John Broadhead, Dan and Ursel Bowditch, Bob Dalgleish, Doug Dobyns, Vic Bell, Wilfried Penker, Lark Clark, Jack Litrell, Jane Nelson, David Phillips, John Beerbower, Robert Orr, Judy Gordon, Brian Dahl, Marianne Bolscher, Judy Letendre, Bayla Schecter, Russ Ellison, Eloise Graham, Andy Whitmore, Karen Kudla, Mike Moon, Margo Meachem, Stu Brinton, Irene Greenburg, Jack Miller, Margo Hearne, Marilyn Miller, Melody Daniels, Paul George, Richard Krieger, Marc Bell, Peter Pollen, Alan Wilson, Dempsey Collison (Chief Skidegate), Nick and Tricia Gessler, Laverne Collinson, John and Janet Foster, Charles F. Bellis, Garth Evans, Jack Woodward, Murray Rankin, Dulcie McCallum, Michael Nicoll, George Yeltatzie, Cathy Anderson, Steve Whipp, Tom Reimchen, Sheila Douglas, Susan Musgrave, Harold Yeltatzie, Tim Boyko, Jimmy Edenshaw, Norm Bentley, Wayne Nelson, Murray Mark, Al Price, Tony Pearse, Lyn Pinkerton, Dennis Rosmini, Ric Helmer, Mary Morris, Hibbey Gren, Graham Lea (MLA-Prince Rupert), Iona Campagnolo (MP-Skeena), Jim Fulton (MP-Skeena), Andrew Thompson, Celia Duthie, David Suzuki, Eileen Nielsen, Catherine de Bucy, Josette Wier, Vicki Sexsmith, Kathryn Kelly, Tom and Tory Schneider, Bill and Wendy McKay, Charlotte Fournier, Bob and Fern Henderson, Miles Richardson Jr., Tom Ellison and the students of B.C.-Quest, Hannelore Evans, Dawn Meredith, Rod Sutton, Calvin Parson, Doug Leach, Bela and Vita Hermanek, Suzanne Soona, Vladimir, Low Tide Blues Band, Skunk Rock, M.I.M.E., Tire Biters, R.L. Smith, B-Side Blues Band, Jim Hart, Geoffrey Ray, Tim Yeomans, Jean-Paul Picard, Dwight Welwood, Don Plumb, Jim Allen, Jim Walker, Bill Ellis, Tim Fitzharris, Peter Hamill, Colleen McCrory, Bob Peart, Al Whitney, Phil Dearden, Kevin McNamee, Michael McPhee, Ray Travers, Janis Kraulis, Betsy Cardell, Lon Sharp, Michael Doherty, Brenda Worden, Rose Hadcock, Maureen McNamara, Alex Doull, Cathey Carr, Bo Martin, Robert Davidson, Robert Wood, John G. Bene, Maurice and Hanne Strong.

To all these and to any whose names — but not whose help — have been forgotten, thank you. HOWA!

Islands Protection Society
May 1984
Queen Charlotte Islands

ABOUT THE AUTHORS

JOHN BROADHEAD has lived on the Queen Charlotte Islands for ten years as an artist, commercial fisherman and carpenter. A long-standing Director of the Islands Protection Society, he also sat on the South Moresby Resource Planning Team. Author of innumerable letters-to-the-editor, designer and producer of posters and publications advocating conservation in South Moresby, he has spent the past two years in Victoria co-ordinating the IPS lobby as well as production of this volume, and doing freelance design work.

WAYNE CAMPBELL attended the University of Victoria, completed graduate studies on birds of prey at the University of Washington, and is presently Associate Curator of the Vertebrate Zoology Division of the British Columbia Provincial Museum. He has published over 200 scientific papers, popular articles and books on British Columbia vertebrates, and is a favorite public speaker on the birds of B.C.

DAVID DENNING graduated from Reed College in Oregon and conducted graduate studies in marine biology at the Universities of Washington and Victoria, and at the Bamfield Marine Station on the west coast of Vancouver Island. He has co-directed nine film productions about marine life, written numerous natural history articles, and is an accomplished nature photographer. He currently works as Field Trip Co-ordinator for the Bamfield Marine Station and serves as a resource naturalist, teacher and photographer for commercial tour companies with natural history orientations on the Pacific coast, especially the Queen Charlotte Islands.

DR. J. BRISTOL FOSTER began his love affair with the Queen Charlotte Islands when he started his doctoral work on the evolution of the land mammals on the Charlottes in the early 1960s. Since then he has served as Professor in charge of graduate student wildlife studies at the University of Nairobi in Kenya, Director of the Provincial Museum in Victoria, British Columbia, and Director of the British Columbia Ecological Reserves Program for the past nine years.

THOM HENLEY was intercepted by the Queen Charlotte Islands half-way through a kayak expedition from Seattle to Alaska. After exploring the South Moresby area and recognizing the international significance, he helped draft the original South Moresby Wilderness Proposal, became a founding member of IPS and has served as spokesman for many years. In 1978 he founded Rediscovery, a natural and cultural heritage program for youth on the Charlottes, and is the Program Director.

JIM POJAR attended the University of Minnesota and received his PhD in botany from the University of British Columbia. For the past nine years he has conducted extensive field work on the Queen Charlottes, first as assistant co-ordinator with the B.C. Ecological Reserves Program, and then in his present capacity as a forest ecologist with the B.C. Forest Service. He has published numerous scientific papers on plant taxonomy, reproductive biology, plant geography, and ecological classifications systems for forests; as well as several popular field guides for plant identification.

BILL REID has, over the past twenty-five years, become one of the masters of the Northwest Coast art style and is an artist with an international reputation. His work rivals the finest ever produced by his Haida forebears and includes wood and argillite carving, silver and gold working, silkscreen print making and sculpture on a monumental scale in a variety of media. In addition, he has created such books as *Out of the Silence* and *Indian Art of the Northwest Coast: A Dialogue on Craftsmanship and Esthetics,* which demonstrate a prose style as carefully polished as some of his best carvings.

PHOTO CREDITS

Jim Allen 37, 131, 147
Frank Boas 39
Robert Bocking 55
Irwin Brodo 58 bc
Wayne Campbell 85, 99 b, 105, 113
Trudy Carson 87, 102, 103, 114 b
Fred Chapman 61, 72, 80
Brent Cook (B.C. Provincial Museum)10, 75, 76 tr, br,
    cl & cr, 88, 90, 91, 93
Gerry Coucill 6-7, 148
Doug Cowell 46 t, 132, 138, 141
David Denning 8, 63, 67 tc & br, 74, 76 tl, bl &
    bc, 78, 79, 81, 83, 84, 97, 105, 112, 116, 144, 151
Adrian Dorst 43 tr, 106, 117
Sheila Douglas 46 b, 67 tl, bl, bc & tr, 130
Ecological Reserves Unit of B.C. 40, 41, 43 tc & br, 69
John Edwards 58 bl & br
Bristol Foster 22, 34, 43 bl, 47, 62, 115, 155
Tricia Guiget 26, 30
Thom Henley 5
Robert Keziere 2, 14, 118
Richard Krieger 29, 31, 42, 48, 51, 54, 57, 58 tl, 65, 68,
    96, 123, 124, 137
John Lamb 127
Jack Litrell 25, 64
Maps, B.C. (Aerial Mapping Branch) 98, 128
Keith Moore 86, 120, 134, 135
Wayne Nelson 114 t
Parks Canada 71
Freeman Patterson 52, 53
Provincial Archives of B.C. 28, 44, 89
Ervio Sian 43 tl & bc, 56, 58 tc & tr, 99 t, 100, 101, 108
Barb Souther 38
Bob Sutherland 60, 104, 110, 143
Art Twomey 45, 82, 94, 126, 152

KEY TO PHOTO CREDITS
t top, b bottom, c centre, l left, r right

159

SUGGESTED READING

Blackman, Margaret. *During My Time, Florence Edenshaw Davidson.* Vancouver: Douglas & McIntyre, 1982.

Bowditch, et. al., eds. *All Alone Stone.* Vol. 4. Masset, Q.C.I.: Islands Protection Society, 1980.

Carefoot, Thomas. *Pacific Seashores: A Guide to Intertidal Ecology.* Vancouver: J.J. Douglas, 1977.

Collison, W.H. *In the Wake of the War Canoe, A Stirring Record of Forty Years.* Reprint. Victoria: Sono Nis Press, 1981.

Dalzell, Kathleen E. *The Queen Charlotte Islands.* 2 vols. Queen Charlotte City, Q.C.I.: Bill Ellis, 1968 (Vol. 1); 1983 (Vol. 2).

de Menil, Adelaide and Reid, Bill. *Out of the Silence.* Toronto: New Press, 1971.

Duff, Wilson. *Impact of White Man.* Part 1. Victoria: B.C. Museum, 1965.

Duff, Wilson and Reid, Bill. *Arts of the Raven: Masterworks by the Northwest Coast Indians.* Vancouver: Vancouver Art Gallery, 1974.

Eckholm, Erik. *Disappearing Species: The Social Challenge.* Worldwatch Paper 22. Washington, D.C.: Worldwatch Institute, 1978.

Ellis, D.W. and Wilson, S. *The Knowledge and Usage of Marine Invertebrates by the Skidegate Haida People of the Queen Charlotte Islands.* Skidegate, Q.C.I.: Queen Charlotte Islands Museum Society, 1981.

Foster, Bristol. *Evolution of the Mammals of the Queen Charlotte Islands.* Occasional Paper No. 14. Victoria: B.C. Provincial Museum, 1965.

Foster, Bristol and Pojar, Jim. *Natural History Theme Study of a Natural Area of Canadian Significance on Queen Charlotte Islands, B.C.* Parks Canada Contract Report 76-209. Ottawa: Parks Canada, 1977.

Harris, Christie. *Raven's Cry.* Toronto: McClelland & Stewart, 1966.

Kozloff, Eugene N. *Seashore Life of the Northern Pacific Coast: An Illustrated Guide to Northern California, Oregon, Washington, and British Columbia.* Vancouver/Toronto: Douglas & McIntyre, 1983.

MacDonald, George F. *Haida Monumental Art: Villages of the Queen Charlotte Islands.* Vancouver: University of British Columbia Press, 1983.

Nichol, Donald J. *Trees, Guardians of the Earth.* Middleton, WI.: The Lorian Association, 1983.

Poole, Francis. *Queen Charlotte Islands: A Narrative of Discovery and Adventure in the North Pacific.* Vancouver, J.J. Douglas, 1982.

Ricketts, Edward and Calvin, Jack. *Between Pacific Tides.* Stanford, CA.: Stanford University Press, 1968.

Simpson, S.L., ed. *The Charlottes, A Journal of the Queen Charlotte Islands.* 4 vols. Skidegate, Q.C.I.: Queen Charlotte Islands Museum Society, 1971, 1973, 1974, 1976.

Simpson, S.L., ed. *Tales from the Queen Charlotte Islands.* 2 vols. Masset, Q.C.I.: Senior Citizens of the Queen Charlotte Islands, 1976, 1979.

Smyly, John and Smyly, Carolyn. *Those Born at Koona.* Vancouver: Hancock House, 1973.

South Moresby Resource Planning Team. *South Moresby, Land Use Alternatives.* Victoria: Queen's Printer, 1983.

Swanton, John R. *Contributions to the Ethnology of the Haida, Jesup North Pacific Expedition.* Volume 5, Part 1. 1905. Reprint. New York: AMS Press, 1975.

Swanton, John R. *Haida Texts and Myths, Skidegate and Dialect.* Bureau of American Ethnology, Bulletin 29. 1905. Reprint. New York: Johnson Reprint, 1970.